Isaac John MacCarthy

Recollections of Rome and other Places

Epoch of the Vatican Council 1869-70

Isaac John MacCarthy

Recollections of Rome and other Places
Epoch of the Vatican Council 1869-70

ISBN/EAN: 9783744764582

Printed in Europe, USA, Canada, Australia, Japan

Cover: Foto ©Lupo / pixelio.de

More available books at **www.hansebooks.com**

RECOLLECTIONS

OF

ROME AND OTHER PLACES.

EPOCH OF THE VATICAN COUNCIL
1869-70.

AFFECTIONATELY DEDICATED
BY
I. J. MacCARTHY, Priest,
TO HIS MANY FRIENDS AND WELL-WISHERS.

Toronto:
HUNTER, ROSE & CO.
1888.

INTRODUCTION.

His Lordship the Right Reverend E. J. Horan, Bishop of Kingston, having been summoned by the Sovereign Pontiff Pius IX.—of blessed memory—to the Œcumenical Council of the Vatican, most graciously invited me to accompany him to Rome—an invitation, it is unnecessary to say, as cheerfully accepted as it was graciously given.

We reached the Eternal City toward the end of November, 1869. I left for home about the last days of April.

During my stay of five months at the centre of Catholicity, I had ample opportunity—and under the most favorable auspices—to visit, time and again, the great monuments of ancient and modern Rome. My excursions were almost daily; and I enjoyed the rare privilege of such a companion as His Lordship, perfectly conversant with the City of the Popes.

In my rambles, I noted down the more interesting objects, that they might be more vividly remembered On my return to Canada, they were found instructive: I was urged to put them into print. I hesitated, knowing how often, how graphically—and how much better than I could hope to do—these things had been described already.

My "Notes" were thrown aside, and almost forgotten amidst the daily busy round of missionary work in the large and laborious parish of Brockville. Returned to Williamstown, I came across them, revised them, and, at the pressing solicitation of friends, consented to give them a lasting form, and in this shape present them to my many friends and well-wishers—hoping they will kindly overlook their many deficiencies, and accept them as a very simple and very unpretending record of what I saw in "Rome and Other Places."

I. J. MacCARTHY,
Priest.

WILLIAMSTOWN, GLENGARRY, ONT.,
  September 8th, 1888,
   Feast of the Nativity of the Blessed Virgin Mary.

CONTENTS.

	PAGE
The Council of the Vatican	9
The Romeward Voyage	10
At Sea	11
Arrival at Liverpool	13
London	14
Arrival at Calais	20
Visit to Amiens Cathedral	22
Paris	22
Lyons	23
Avignon	26
Marseilles	29
Arrival at Rome	31
St. Peter's	34
The Council	36
St. Mary Major's	40
St. Paul's on the Ostian Way	42
The Pantheon	44
The Etruscan Statue on the Capitoline Hill	47
Basilica of St. John of Lateran	49
My Diary	52
Adieu to Rome	133
Pisa	135
Sienna	136
Florence	137

Contents.

	PAGE
Padua	138
Venice	139
Milan	140
From Verona to Munich	142
Cologne	145
Dover	147
Edinburgh	147
Inverness	148
Glasgow	150
Home, Sweet Home!	151

Notes on the Mission of St. Francis Xavier	152
Rev. Father MacCarthy's Jubilee	157
Removal of Father MacCarthy from Brockville	165
Address of his Parishioners previous to his departure	166
Opinions of the Local Press on the Matter	168
Signatures appended to the requisition to Right Reverend Bishop Cleary, from Brockville	170
"Dies Iræ, Dies Illa," as translated by Father MacCarthy	177
"The Cradle Song of the Blessed Virgin," translated from the Latin, by Father MacCarthy	179
Instructions for St. Patrick's Day, March 17th, 1885	180
Notes on the Nativity of the Blessed Virgin Mary	199
Address from the Parish of Williamstown, to Rev. Father MacCarthy	204
FAREWELL: A Poem, from the pupils of the Congregation of Notre Dame	206

RECOLLECTIONS OF ROME,

AND OTHER PLACES.

1869-70.

EPOCH OF THE VATICAN COUNCIL.

CHAPTER I.

I.

THE greatest of Pontiffs had spoken; the immortal Pius IX. had summoned the Patriarchs, Priests, Archbishops and Bishops of the Catholic world, in communion with the Holy See, to meet in the Eternal City for the most important event of the nineteenth century, the Council of the Vatican.

More than eighteen hundred years ago, the first Pope, Simon Bar-Jona, Peter, the chosen of Christ, the Prince of the Apostolic College, in an humble chamber held the first Æcumenical Council and decreed: "It hath seemed good to the Holy Ghost and to us, not to lay any further burden upon you, our brethren of the Gentiles in Antioch, in Syria and Cilicia, than that you abstain from things offered to idols, from blood, from strangled meats and fornication."

As the first, to whom—"all power in heaven and upon earth was granted"—so the two hundred and sixty-

second, successor, to whom the same power is continued:
—"Lo! I am with you all days, unto the consummation of the world"—(St. Matthew)—finds, that for the wants of the Spouse of Christ, those whom the Holy Ghost had placed to govern the Church of God, should be called together; and the summons goes forth—*Urbi et Orbi*—and from the four winds of heaven, from the extremities of the earth, the princes of God's people hasten to the city of the seven hills, obedient to the voice of the Supreme Pastor of souls, the Vicar of the incarnate God; thus acknowledging that Peter lives in his successors, and that—" ubi Petrus, ibi ecclesia "—where Peter is there is the Church.

II..

QUEBEC.

The 23rd of October, 1869, their Lordships the Archbishop of Quebec, the Bishops of Kingston, St. Hyacinthe, Three-Rivers, and Idaho, U.S.T., accompanied by several priests, their companions, after the "Itinerarium," during which, in the grand old cathedral of the ancient capital, now raised to the dignity of a Basilica, by His Holiness Leo XIII., at the foot of the gorgeous altar, they implored the Divine mercy and the protection of the immaculate Mother on their Romeward voyage, left for for the steamer, accompanied by the clergy, an immense concourse of citizens, the Professors of the University of Laval, and the students of the Petit-Séminaire, headed by their splendid band. It was a bleak October morning, cold, but not enough to cool the enthusiasm of the assembled thousands, who waited until our noble ship weighed anchor, and loudly cheered the venerable prelates as they raised their hands to bless them, while the splendid vessel—the Nestorian—majestically left the harbor. While in Quebec, we were the guests of His Grace, Mgr Baillargeon who, with his venerable clergy, entertained us most regally. The day before our departure, the gentlemen of the Seminary gave a grand dinner in honor of the assembled prelates. Bishop Horan and I said mass in the ancient chapel of the Ursulines.

III.

AT SEA.

Our trip across the Atlantic was more than usually pleasant. We had some pretty rough weather; indeed, some of the roughest ever experienced in the Gulf of St. Lawrence, and yet, seldom was made better headway.

As might be expected, the first few days many were very sea-sick, and no doubt some of them felt like the Irishman who said, when he first went aboard ship, he feared they would all go to the bottom; but when he got sick, he was afraid they would not.

Sunday morning, the second day out, we had the great happiness of assisting at the adorable Sacrifice of the Mass, a rare privilege at sea, and upon two other occasions during the passage. His Lordship Bishop Horan was the celebrant, and the Vicar-General, now the Cardinal Archbishop of Quebec, the assistant.

Nothing can be imagined grander, more-impressive, than Mass on the broad bosom of the ocean. It is true there is the absence of all that pomp, that ritualistic splendor, that generally surrounds this, the greatest of all the ordinances of religion. We miss the magnificence of the grand cathedral, or the charms of the simple, yet beautiful, village church; but on the other hand, the very want of them reminds us of our own nothingness, and the mind, recalling the perils of the deep, is more than usually absorbed in the contemplation of the dread Majesty of Him whom the winds and the waves obey, and who ever guides and guards His children. Never shall we forget the impressions of those happy mornings; the consolation of hearing Mass; the sense of security one felt as we left the little chamber on deck where, around the temporary altar, we had been privileged to assist at a mass on sea. Going thirteen knots an hour. Sun set to-day at four o'clock.

Our fellow-passengers were most agreeable, and after a few days, when the "sick were restored to health," we enjoyed the remainder of the voyage amazingly. Entertainments were given occasionally, that helped much to relieve the monotony of the trip, and afforded genuine amusement.

Sunday evening, nine days out, we espied the lights on Tory Island, and at ten o'clock entered Lough Foyle, when a small boat, a tender, came to take the mail and passengers for Ireland.

Though the night was exceedingly dark, we crowded on deck, anxious for a glimpse of the land of our fathers. All we could see were the lights glimmering in the distance; yet, the very fact that we were in presence of the the dear old sod, for the first time, afforded us a pleasure that is still a pleasure to look back to.

Here, rockets were fired from the ship, producing a beautiful effect in the profound darkness. The next day was intensely disagreeable; about ten p.m., we reached the large and wealthy city of Liverpool, ranking next to London in commercial enterprise and importance.

This morning we had again the happiness of assisting at the Holy Sacrifice, Mgr. Horan officiating.

IV.

ARRIVAL AT LIVERPOOL.

Our first day in Liverpool was "All-Souls," and our first visit in this great city was to the beautiful Gothic Church of St. Vincent de Paul, to return thanks to God for our safe and happy voyage. This fine church was under the care of the Very Rev. Canon O'Rielly, now the venerable bishop of the diocese.

The canon received us with that courtesy for which he is so distinguished, kindly exhibiting to us the rich and costly ornaments, and other interesting objects.

Taking our leave of this worthy gentleman, we visited the famous docks, which extend for miles, then crowded with vessels from all parts of the world. About twenty-five thousand ships annually enter this port.

Liverpool boasts of many fine buildings. St. George's Hall is one of the finest, a noble structure; the interior is adorned with many beautiful statues of the purest marble, costly paintings, and contains a magnificent organ.

If in Liverpool there is found immense wealth, there is also immense misery. During the few days we spent there we beheld more poverty, more abject wretchedness, than during the next six months on the continent. As crime is generally the outcome of great poverty, no doubt great wickedness must prevail. We supped one evening at Dr. Kelly's, a brother of the late Very Rev'd. Oliver Kelly, formerly parish priest of Saint Francis Xaviers, Brockville.

V.

From Liverpool we went to London, two hundred and thirty-six miles distant. The route between the two cities is charming, passing by thriving towns, villages, and villas, in a most delightful country. We passed a week in the great metropolis, during which we visited its most interesting monuments :—Westminster Abbey, St. Paul's Cathedral, the British Museum, the new Houses of Parliament, and many other interesting places, well worthy the attention of the tourist, and which, of course, no one fails to see.

In Westminster Abbey, that great creation of Catholic genius, one scarcely knows what to admire most. The architecture is of the purest gothic, and the many noble monuments raised to the illustrious dead, make it a place of absorbing interest.

As Catholics, of the shrines that most excited our veneration were those of Saint Edward the Confessor, which occupies the centre of the magnificent chapel, dedicated to the memory of this glorious king, the last of the Saxon race; and our pity and respect, that of the martyred queen, the beautiful, but unfortunate Marie Stuart.

As we passed the former, we pressed our lips reverently to the holy shrine; and at the latter, breathed a requiem for the murdered queen.

This tomb is in the south side of Henry Seventh's chapel, and the grand monument erected by the miserable James —Mary's son—to the murderess of his mother, stands in the north aisle of the same.

Needless to say, the very sight of it filled us with horror, and we hastened by, scarcely glancing at the fulsome inscription engraved upon it. His lordship and myself again visited the Abbey; one never wearies gazing upon this grand old Catholic Church. The celebrated stone upon which the Kings of Scotland sat at their coronation is here, and fixed in the chair upon which sit the Sovereigns of England on the day of their coronation.

St. Paul's Cathedral, the great and solitary boast of Protestantism, is worthy of a better cause. Indeed we much think were the apostle of the Gentiles to visit it, he should fail to recognize it for a Christian temple.

A portion of it is used for "divine service"; and the rest looks as heathenish as can well be imagined. Statues of "History", "Fame", "Victory", "Britannia", are met on every side; and give this, otherwise splendid church, the appearance of what the Pantheon might have been in the days of the pagan emperors of Rome. The other visits that filled up our time were to the Crystal Palace, the Zoological Gardens, the Parks, and some of the Catholic Churches. We particularly admired Bishop Grant's splendid cathedral, one of Pugin's best, on the Surry side of the Thames.

One morning we saw Her Majesty on her way to open the new Black Friars bridge, and the Holborn viaduct. She bowed, we cannot say gracefully, but repeatedly and good naturedly, to her lieges, as she drove along; some of whom, if we may judge from the muttered expressions, were anything but charmed with the show and pomp of royalty, while many wanted work, and consequently—bread.

In London we had the pleasure of meeting the Rev. Angus McDonald, of Prince Edward's Island, an old Quebec seminary acquaintance, and with whom I had the pleasure to travel home, on my return from Rome.

VI.

Said mass at Spanish Place Church; and about four o'clock, afternoon, with Mgrs. Horan and Lootens, drove to St. George's. Canon Daniel, afterwards Bishop of Southwark, received us with the greatest kindness, and had the church lighted up that we might see its beauties to advantage.

Tuesday, Nov. 9th, saw us on our way to Dover. This romantic old town is one of the chief seaports of England —directly opposite the coast of France. It is built in a valley between lofty chalk hills which, especially when reflecting the rays of the sun, present a most picturesque appearance. The great object of attraction in town is its ancient castle. This magnificent specimen of the Norman stronghold stands on a lofty eminence overlooking the channel.

From the northern limit, 468 feet above the level of the sea, we have a splendid view of the town, a great portion of Kent, and far out to sea.

It was growing dark as we left the castle, and, in the distance, we could see distinctly the lights along the French shore. Whether considered under the Roman, Saxon or Norman rule, no fortress in England combines more historical associations than this ancient pile.

Connected with the castle, is the church of St. Mary, said to have been built in the fourth century. It is now in the cruciform style, accommodating about six hundred persons.

No one can visit Dover without being struck by what is called 'Shakespeare's Cliff,' named from the poet, who describes it in his celebrated tragedy of King Lear:—

> "There is a cliff, whose high and bending head
> Looks fearfully on the confined deep.
>   How fearful
> And dizzy 'tis, to cast one's eyes so low !
> The crows and choughs that wing the midway air
> Show scarce as large as beetles ; half way down
> Hangs one that gathers samphire—dreadful trade !
> Methinks he looks no bigger than his head ;
> The fishermen that walk upon the beach
> Appear like mice ; and you tall anchoring bark
> Diminished to her cock ; her cock a buoy
> Almost too small for sight. The murmuring surge,

> That on the unnumbered pebbles chafes,
> Cannot be heard so high. I'll look no more,
> Lest my brain turn, and the deficient sight,
> Topple down headlong."

Next morning, after mass in the small but pretty church, we drove over to Canterbury, through a lovely section of the country.

The morning was delightful, the air bracing, and upon all sides the landscape enchanting. England was called "Merry England;" well might it be called beautiful England, for it well deserves the name.

Canterbury is situated in a valley on the Stour. Though very ancient it is still a fine city, with a population of some thirty-five thousand souls (1869).

The famous cathedral, like all the great ecclesiastical monuments, was built when England was Catholic.

The daily afternoon service, corresponding to the Complins of yore, was going on as we entered; and having listened for a few moments to the truly delicious strains echoing through the spacious empty church, we went to lunch, intending to return when "divine service" should be ended.

Returning, we were shown through this majestic pile. Here St. Thomas à Beckett, the defender of the liberties of the Church, was murdered at the vesper hour by the minions of a base, tyrannical king. We knelt upon the very stones which had once been purpled with his life's-blood; and we prayed that, like him, we might be ever faithful and true to Holy Mother Church.

The spot where, in holier and happier times, stood his sacred shrine, was pointed out to us. The steps of marble leading to it, as well as the surrounding pavement, are hollowed by the knees of the numberless pilgrims who came to claim his intercession at his hallowed tomb.

The "Lady's Chapel," of course, no longer exists; we saw where it was once, when its bishops were worthy of being enrolled among the saints of God. Alas! alas! to think of England, once a truly Catholic nation, and now so sadly fallen from her high estate; carried to and fro by every wind of doctrine, seeking for rest and yet finding none. Let us hope, however, since the blood of the martyrs is the seed of the Church, that the blood of the martyred à Beckett and of many others put to death in that fair land for the faith of their fathers, and consequently no less martyrs than he, may plead powerfully before God and obtain that the English people, who need only to be Catholic to be the greatest people on earth, may return to the House of their Father, and find peace and rest in the "one fold of the one Shepherd."

Returned to Dover by train, a distance of sixteen miles, and spent a most pleasant evening with Captain and Mrs. Moore and her amiable and accomplished sister, Miss T——, then on a visit from Canada. The rev. the parish priest, and a distinguished convert from Anglicanism—now a Catholic clergyman—dined with us. This gentleman wore the soutane, cincture, Roman-collar—and indeed seemed rather proud of his ecclesiastical costume. We again said mass in the pretty church, St. Mary's.

CHAPTER II.

I.

THE morning after our visit to Canterbury we bade adieu to Dover and friends, whose genuine hospitality we shall not easily forget. Poor Captain Moore died since— on his way from China. He was, indeed, one of nature's true gentlemen!

We reached Calais in about two hours. The passage of the channel was exceedingly unpleasant. A high wind, a boisterous crossing, and as usual, many awfully seasick.

The harbor has a very imposing appearance, defended by several small forts : a large quay, with its long wooden piers, stretches far into the sea. The entrance to the harbor was fearful. Five men stood at the helm, so difficult was it to manage the packet. Calais presents the appearance of a goodly town ; it is constructed principally of brick. It enjoys a brisk trade, chiefly in the manufacture of cotton and silk lace. As every one knows it was this place of which Queen Mary said, on learning that it was lost to England, "After death, its name shall be found written upon my heart." A truly royal sentiment, right royally expressed.

Here are some fine churches. Notre-Dame, eleventh century, boasts of beautiful stained windows, and paintings by Rubens and Vandyke—real master-pieces.

Our next stopping-place was the old town of Boulogne-sur-mer, where we passed the night. After breakfast, the following morning, we visited the principal churches of the city, the most remarkable being Notre-Dame, erected by Monsignor Haffringue, to whom we had the honor of an introduction. The altars vie with some of the most beautiful known, and would grace the finest temple on earth.

The grand altar, the gift of the Roman Prince Torlonia, is composed of the rarest marbles and mosaics, at a cost of five hundred thousand francs. On the brow of the hill stands the little famous chapel of the Boulogne fishermen, overlooking the sea. It is quaint, and very small, but contains some good paintings : its walls are hung with *ex votos*, in gratitude to Mary, the Star of the sea, to whose all powerful protection many owe their rescue from a watery grave. It was a touching sight, the fervent piety of the women and children who crowded this holy place, praying for husbands and fathers, far away on the deep.

We knelt with them at the foot of our Lady's altar, to implore her care ; and, ere we left, lit a taper for ourselves and the loved ones at home.

An object of great curiosity in Boulogne, is the celebrated column, commemorating the intended invasion of England by Napoleon. It is magnificent, as well as its surroundings.

It was here he distributed the decorations to the " Grande Armée." From this lofty eminence, the view of the sea and country is superb.

Our visit to Boulogne was particularly enjoyable, the

weather being delightful, and contrasting wonderfully with the dark days we had spent in London.

II.

In the afternoon we reached Amiens, celebrated for its glorious old cathedral, 420 feet in length, and admittedly one of the noblest in Europe.

The city has a fine appearance; the streets are spacious, and the places of business splendid. The gare, or depot, is immense, and is kept in first-class style..

Our stay here was short; merely enough to visit the chief point of interest—the cathedral—and to see the principal parts of the city.

From Amiens to Paris, the distance is eighty-one miles. The journey occupied three hours and forty minutes—rather slow travelling by train.

It was near midnight as we entered the loveliest city in Europe—the rendezvous of the pleasure seekers of the world.

Paris is built on both sides of the Seine, the river running from east to west; its circumference is fifteen of our miles. Put up at the Hotel, "Bon Lafontaine." Tolerably good house; charges very high.

As usual, next day our first visits were to the churches, most of which are very grand, and very numerous.

The world-renowned Notre-Dame, built in the twelfth century, with its gorgeous towers, and its noble entrances, splendidly wrought, is a temple of vast proportions and great magnificence.

The gallery is supported by 297 pillars, elegantly sculptured, and the choir, which is flanked by one hundred and twenty, is rich with choice paintings and exquisite carving.

We assisted at vespers, complins and benediction of the Blessed Sacrament, and regretted to see so meagre an attendance.

The chanting, accompanied by the great organ, was delightful; in perfect harmony with the place. We said mass at St. Sulpice, and paid a visit to the Venerable Superior-General.

In Paris, His Lordship and I called upon the Very Rev. Father Hecker, Superior of the Paulists, New York, and had the honor of meeting His Grace the Most Rev. Dr. Connolly, the distinguished and whole-souled Archbishop of Halifax, my native place. We visited the Hotel des Invalides, famous as the last resting-place of the great Napoleon, and many other interesting sights, too many to mention. The *Pantheon*, now called Saint Genevieve, is one of the most faultless edifices in Paris, but unfortunately is dishonored by the remains of the infidel, Voltaire, who lies beneath it. The tomb of the holy shepherdess is in St. Etienne's du Mont, where Archbishop Sibour was assassinated.

III.

LYONS.

Lyons is the chief manufacturing city in France. We reached it on the evening of the 16th November. It is built at the conjunction of the Saone and the Rhone, is a place of vast traffic, and in every respect a city of very great importance.

The great square, Louis the Grand, is renowned throughout the continent. It is beautifully designed, planted with fine trees and adorned with a superb equestrian statue of the fourteenth Louis, most resembling those seen in the vestibule of St. Peter's, at Rome, and which are erected to the memory of Constantine and Charlemagne.

Lyons is justly proud of her public library, with its 150,000 volumes, and 2,400 manuscripts. We did not count them.

The cathedral, dedicated to the beloved disciple, is of the twelfth century, gothic, and adorned with windows of stained glass, ancient and rich, producing that "dim religious light"—so conducive to piety and prayer, and so much vaunted by the lovers of the beautiful. The bell weighs 20,000 lbs; a great curiosity to the visitor is an old astronomical clock, with figures of our Lord and the twelve apostles, dating from 1598.

The Sacristan most obligingly allowed us to inspect the treasures of the church, some of the most valuable in Europe.

The vestments are gorgeous. One cope of cloth of gold cost twenty-five thousand francs. The embroidery is simply indescribable.

Here we saw ornaments once belonging to Cardinal Fesch, and a most costly and elaborate ostensorium, presented to His Eminence by his nephew, the first Napoleon.

What interested us much more, was a chasuble wrought

by the ladies of the court of Louis XIII. for Saint Vincent de Paul.

Among the relics which we were privileged to venerate was the saint's heart: a bone of St. Irenaeus, Bishop of Lyons; and, above all, a thorn of our blessed Lord's crown, a particle of the wood of the true cross, and of the holy winding sheet in which His sacred body was laid in the tomb.

Twice during my stay in Lyons I climbed the heights of Fourvières, to celebrate the holy sacrifice at the shrine of Our Lady, which is covered with *ex votos*.

The Lyonese have immense devotion to the Mother of God, under the title of Notre Dame de Fourvières. To her powerful intercession with her divine Son, they ascribe the deliverance of their city from cholera, immediately after their public vow, made in her honor. From Fourvières, the ascent to which is most fatiguing, on a clear day, may be seen the celebrated Mont Blanc, distant about one hundred miles. The Hotel Dieu—a vast hospital—is served by nuns who wear a very quaint costume. We were told the order had existed for upwards of 700 years. Nowhere did we see members of so many religious orders, so many diverse costumes.

Truly Lyons is the city of Mary, and perhaps the most truly Catholic of all the cities of fair France.

At Fourvières I had some masses said by the rev. clergy, and some tapers lit at the holy shrine, for my intentions. His Eminence, Cardinal de Bonald, was the Archbishop of Lyons (1869). We had to forego paying our respects to his lordship, who happened to be very ill at the time.

IV.

AVIGNON.

Three hours and a-half, by train, brought us to Avignon, the principal city of the Vaucluse, on the Rhone, and seventy-five miles north of Marseilles. After dining, we visited the Hotel Dieu, built in 1351, under the French Popes, which is under the care of the cloistered nuns, Sisters of St. Joseph, the same order as those of Montreal and Kingston. These devoted women were driven from this ancient convent in 1790, and again, in our own days —1845. From the Hotel Dieu we went to the old church and palace of the popes, who resided here from 1305 till 1378.

In the papal church, built in the eleventh century, are seen the tombs of Benedict XIII. and John XXII.; the latter of the whitest marble, and a masterpiece of art. In the sanctuary, still remains the pontifical throne, also of marble. Several excellent portraits of the popes, and some very good paintings, grace the walls of this historic church. Clement V. was the first—Gregory XI. who died in Rome—the last of the popes who resided at Avignon. In all seven, not counting two anti-popes.

The papal palace, now used for a barrack and prison, is a huge quadrangular structure, having four large towers, which give it the appearance of a gigantic fortress.

The palace gardens, now a public promenade, are beautiful, and from them, high above the river, is taken in a splendid view of the Rhone and the adjacent country.

At a short distance is seen the bridge, now in ruins, said to have been constructed by St. Benezet, in 1177-88.

A legend is attached to this interesting ruin. It says, that presenting himself to the authorities, this holy man assured them that he had been commissioned by God to have a bridge built there.

The governor, naturally incredulous, said to him: To prove the truth of what you say, carry that—pointing to an immense rock—to the place. The Saint did it, and the bridge was built. It is not used at present, but sufficient remains to show it was no ordinary work. The population was 35,000. A dull place.

Sunday morning we said mass in the beautiful chapel of the Hotel Dieu, and after breakfast visited the wards of the hospital, in which there were one hundred and fifty patients, and which were kept, as only nuns can keep them. The good sisters had adopted a young negress, who had been sold four times as a slave. We dined with the Rev. Chaplain, a polished, courteous, and highly accomplished priest, and then proceeded to Nimes, so deservedly celebrated for its antiquarian remains.

This is indeed an elegant city. One-third of the population is Huguenot, and we must admit, nowhere in France did we see the Sunday, at least so far as appearances go, so strictly observed. A noble Coliseum, second only to the Vespasian, and said to have been built by the Romans, with sixty outlets, and accommodating twenty-five thousand spectators, is one of the very great attractions to Nimes.

The temple of the goddess Diana is still well preserved after such a lapse of time. The place whence the Sibyl uttered her oracles is pointed out to the tourist.

Here is found the famous Maison-Carrée, or Square House, acknowledged as perhaps the most perfect specimen of Corinthian architecture. This house, built by Augustus for Antoninus Pius, is at present used as a public museum, and a rare one it is. Near the temple of Diana wells up a most copious fountain, the source of which seems a mystery, supplying the city with water, a most fortunate thing, for this year (1869), no rain had fallen for eight months, preventing the usual agricultural industries. The grounds about the fountain are carefully laid out, not the least of their ornaments being four colossal statues, allegorical of the four seasons. The saintly Pius VII. in the days of his exile honored Nimes with a visit.

So great was the multitude that thronged the way of the Vicar of Christ, it took five hours to pass a few acres. His Holiness granted an indulgence to the city, being deeply impressed by the demonstrations of love, respect, and veneration manifested by the people for his sacred character. Asked by Fouché how he had found France, "Blessed be heaven!" replied the Pope, " we have crossed it amid a kneeling population. How far were we from believing such to be the state of France."

V.

MARSEILLES.

It was night when we got to Marseilles—merely in time to reach the packet for Italy, consequently we saw, and that by gas-light, but little of the city.

From the deck of the vessel, even by night, it presents a fine appearance, rising high above the waters of the Mediterranean. The moon shone fitfully through the clouds, portending foul weather, which unfortunately for us proved too true.

The vessel was crowded. On board was a very large number of passengers, far too many to be comfortable, including His Eminence the Cardinal Archbishop of Besancon, twenty-six bishops from Europe, Asia, Africa and America, besides a host of priests.

The weather was dreadful ; a fierce storm came on. The passage from Marseilles to Civita Vecchia, which is generally made in thirty-six hours, occupied three days and four nights.

It was reported that our vessel was lost. Twice we were obliged to seek refuge ; once in the harbor of Elba, famous for the residence of Napoleon, in 1815 ; and again, in the Porto d' Hercule, where we had the gratification of laying at anchor all night. Friday morning at ten o'clock, we steamed into the port of Civita Vecchia and soon, for the first time, stood upon the shores of lovely Italy, the land of painting, of music, and of song ; the home of all that is grand and beautiful ; the fairest of God's earth ;

the centre of Catholicity—the home of the Pontiff, of the successor of Peter, of the Vicar of Jesus Christ, of the Supreme Head of the Catholic Church. We lunched at the palace of the Bishop, who was also governor of the city, and at four o'clock took the train for Rome, arriving about 8 p.m.

At the depot we found carriages, by order of His Holiness, waiting to convey the bishops to their hotels. We secured excellent quarters at the "Minerva," one of the finest public houses in the city, and but a moment's walk from the celebrated Dominican Church, known as Santa Maria Sopra Minerva.

CHAPTER III.

ROME.

I.

" ROME is situated in the centre nearly of the Campagna, that undulating tract which lies between the Sabine Apennines and the Cimenian range of hills on the north, and the low country extending along the shores of the Mediterranean on the west. Its nearest point in a straight line from the sea-coast is thirteen miles. The modern city is built in the plain which lies on each bank of the Tiber, and on the slopes of the seven hills which formed such well-known features in the topography of ancient Rome. The height of these hills, within the circuit of the present walls, varies from one hundred and twenty to one hundred and eighty feet above the river. The Tiber divides the city into two very unequal portions, traversing it from north to south in a winding course of about three miles. On the left bank, the Pincian, Quirinal, Viminal, and Capitoline hills form a kind of amphitheatre, encircling the irregular flat of the Campus Martius. On the right bank of the Tiber lies the narrow flat which contains the districts of the Borgo and Trastevere. It is bounded on the west by a ridge of hills. The principal eminences of this ridge within the walls are the Vatican and the Janiculum, which preserve nearly unaltered their ancient names.

Beyond the walls, the picturesque Monte Mario, with its villas and cypress plantations, may be considered the continuation of this elevated ridge on the north, and the hill of Sta. Passera beyond the Porta Portese on the south. The Trastevere and the Borgo are united by the street of the Lungara, built by Sixtus V. in the level space between the Tiber and the declivity of the Janiculum." *The walls of Rome*, including those of the Trastevere and the Vatican, are from twelve to thirteen miles in circuit.

My first day in Rome was Saturday, a day sacred to the Blessed Virgin, and my first visit, accidentally, to one of her churches, St. Mary of the Angels, constructed of a portion of the baths of Diocletian. Called at the Propaganda in the evening with Mgr., who had business with Cardinal Barnabo.

This church, outwardly not at all remarkable, within is perfectly exquisite. It has fine paintings; among others an immense fresco, transported in one piece from St. Peter's—a wonderful undertaking.

Here is St. Bruno's statue in white marble, considered one of the most perfect of the modern school. It is the work of the French sculptor Hudon. So true to life is it, that one of the Popes said, "It would speak, did not the rule prescribe silence." A great and well-merited eulogium.

By a side door opening from the church we entered the cloisters of the monastery, and were most kindly received by one of the venerable Carthusian fathers.

Here the exhibition of Christian art was to be held

in February, and no more suitable place could have been selected.

In the gardens of this noble convent three stately cypress trees planted (now, 1887) three hundred and ninety years ago, by Michael Angelo, were pointed out to us.

Soon after quitting the monastery we had the good luck of meeting the Pope and got his blessing, a presage of God's blessing during our sojourn in the city of the Vicar of His Son.

My first mass in Rome was on Sunday, and celebrated in the church of the Dominicans, commonly called the Minerva.

Upon this spot Pompey, wishing to immortalise his Asiatic victories, had dedicated a temple to the goddess of war and wisdom.

This church, partly Gothic, a rare thing in Rome, was lately restored by the good fathers at a cost of half a million of francs.

Under the high altar reposes the body of Saint Catharine of Sienna, one of the most illustrious of the Dominican saints.

Here on the festival of the Annunciation, His Holiness holds a papal chapel, and gives dowries to poor young women, some of whom marry, while others, more fortunate, consecrate themselves to God in the silence of the cloister.

It was the first Sunday of Advent, and the "Quarante Ore" at St. Peter's.

Taking a hurried breakfast, I hastened to the great Basilica, and arrived in good time for the procession of the Most Holy Sacrament. His Holiness, over whom was held a gorgeous canopy, carried the "Holy of Holies,' accompanied by some three hundred bishops, cardinals, the noble guard, the diplomatic corps, and all the great officers of his household.

The brave Zouaves, whom His Holiness always loved to honor, lined the way of the cortege, and at least twenty thousand people must have been present on this sublime occasion, and bent in lowly adoration, as Jesus Christ, present in the Sacrament of His love, was borne along to be enthroned on the high altar of the greatest temple ever raised by the hand of man to the worship of the living God.

> "But thou of temples old, or altars new,
> Standest above—with nothing like to thee—
> Worthiest of God, the holy and the true.
> Since Zion's desolation, when that He
> Forsook the former city, what could be,
> Of earthly structures, in his Honor piled,
> Of a sublimer aspect? Majesty,
> Power, Glory, Strength, and Beauty all are aisled
> In this eternal ark of worship undefiled."
> —BYRON.

II.

The great attraction for the traveller on arriving in Rome is St. Peter's, which has been so truly designated as—"the most glorious structure that has ever been applied to the use of religion."

In the year 90, Saint Anacletus, ordained by, and successor of, the prince of the apostles, erected on the present site of the great Basilica an oratory, in honor of Saint Peter.

It is uncertain whether it was on the Janiculum, or near the circus of Nero, on the Vatican, that the apostle was put to death. Be this as it may, it is certain his sacred relics were deposited here ; and hence the veneration ever afterward attached to this hallowed spot.

In the year 324, Constantine, the first Christian emperor, laid the foundation of the temple which he, in thanksgiving to God for the gift of faith, desired to raise over the tomb of the " Fisherman."

This grand imperial structure lasted eleven centuries and a-half ; the admiration of the Christian world.

In the year 1450, it threatened ruin, and the reigning Pontiff, Nicholas V., determined on rebuilding. From this date, till 1626, when the consecration took place, one hundred and seventy-six years elapsed ; and, if we include the completing the sacristy under Pius VI. we shall have 330 years, during which forty-three popes reigned.

At the close of the 17th century, Carlo Maderno estimated its cost at 46,800,428 scudi—£10,000,000 sterling, not including the sacristy—900,000 scudi.

Repairs annually amount to thirty thousand dollars. Like almost all who see St. Peter's for the first time, I must admit I was rather disappointed.

It by no means presents the immensity we had imagined ; it seems strikingly smaller than it is really ; a fact accounted for by its wonderfully exact proportions. However, after a few visits, its vastness grows upon us. The length is $613\frac{1}{2}$—English feet.

The width of the nave and side aisles, including the pilasters that separate them, is $197\frac{3}{4}$ feet. The extreme length of the transepts, from end to end, is 446½ feet. The height of the nave over the doors is 152½ feet, and of the dome, from the pavement to the top of the cross outside, 448 feet.

Volumes would be needed to detail the splendor, beauty and loveliness of this divinest of temples. It contains forty-seven altars, each magnificent, when we consider the wealth of art that surrounds them. Indeed, had the popes done little else, the world would be indebted to them for this, the grandest conception of the mind of man.

III.

THE COUNCIL.

Here, St. Peter's, on the 8th day of December, 1869, festival of the Immaculate Conception, was opened the Council of the Vatican, the nineteenth general Council of the Church of God; assuredly, in whatever light we may regard it, the greatest the world has ever seen.

The day was most unpropitious, heavy rain and wind; yet a vast multitude had assembled early at St. Peter's anxious to behold the great pageant.

On the grand altar, beneath the " wondrous dome," the most adorable Sacrament was exposed, and thousands knelt in prayer before it, imploring the divine blessing upon the important work about to be inaugurated on that auspicious day. The great door of St. Peter's is thrown open; all eyes turn to it, and the Cross—the sign of the Son of Man—appears above the heads of the kneeling multitude.

Following come the six hundred bishops representing the Catholic world, and the grandest, most sublime, most imposing procession ever beheld within the sacred Basilica, is closed by the Vicar of Christ borne on his throne, while from the tribune above the great door, come strains of the most ravishing, unearthly melody.

Before the high altar the Pontiff descends and, prostrate, adores his divine Lord in the mystery of His love, and then entered the Aula and assisted at the solemn Mass offered for the success of the Council.

IV.

The most noble of Rome's noble ruins is the Coliseum, also known as the Flavian Amphitheatre, owing its existence to the Emperors of the Flavian family. Begun in the year 82 by Vespasian, it was dedicated by Titus in the year of our Lord 80; ten years after the taking by the latter of Jerusalem.

Tradition tells us its architect was Gaudentius, a Christian and a martyr, whose relics now rest within one of the most ancient churches—Sta. Martina and Sta. Luca—in the Forum.

Thousands of captive Jews were employed in this work. Up to the year 523, the blood of wild beasts, and of gladiators little less ferocious, flowed freely on its soil. This enormous construction is built principally of stone called Travertine, with much brick work in the interior.

The form is ellipticle and the style Doric, Ionic and Corinthian. It has four storeys; the height of the outer wall is 157 feet, it accommodates one hundred thousand spectators.

Few places in the eternal city possess greater interest for the Christian than these wonderful ruins. There, thousands of our brethren, in the first ages of the Church, shed their life's blood for the faith we this day hold.

Here the glorious Martyr St. Ignatius, bishop of Antioch, was torn to pieces by lions; and here Eustache, his wife, their two children, and the noble virgins Martina, Tatiana and Prisca; the Senator Julius, the Bishops Alexander and Elutherius; the young Persian princes, Abdon and Sennen, and countless others gladly suffered death for the defence of the truths preached by the humble fisherman of Galilee. Attempts were made, fortunately unsuccessful, to make of this place a manufactory.

In 1750, the learned and saintly Benedict XIV. consecrated it to the glorious martyrs put to death therein. It was then the Via Crucis, or stations of the cross, were erected, and Saint Leonard of Port Maurice established the pious confraternity which, every Sunday and Friday, two hours before the Ave Maria, performs here the touching exercise that recalls so vividly the Saviour's painful journey to Calvary. More than once while in Rome did I make the stations within these sacred precincts; and never shall I forget my impressions when assisting at this sublime devotion, in the afternoon of Good Friday. Thousands thronged the holy place, and, headed by the venerable bishop of Beauvais, performed the way of the cross. It was a sight for angels to look upon; 'a sight that must have given joy to the sainted heroes who ages ago had suffered and had died on that vast arena, now pressed by the knees of devout worshipers from all parts of the world, who, while they meditated on the humiliations and death of the King of martyrs, blessed God that in Him, others, almost innumerable, had found grace and strength to suffer and to die.

On the north of the Coliseum still stands a portion of the fountain called the Meta Sudans. It was most probably for the use of the gladiators after their combats in the amphitheatre. For the botanist, the coliseum has special attractions: an English physician who resided in Rome, assures us that four hundred species of plants are found growing on its walls.

By this time, another may be added to the list,—a right rev. friend from one of America's wildest regions, having sown seed of some, peculiar to the Rocky mountains.

Not far from the Coliseum, at the entrance of the Via di San. Gregori, is seen the arch erected by the Senate and Roman people in honor of Constantine, victorious over Maxentius and Licinius. It is composed of three arches; is built of marble, with fine fluted columns in the Corinthian order, and is covered with exquisite bas reliefs. Critics say, as a work of art, it is far from perfect; yet the majority of visitors will view it with much pleasure and satisfaction.

We returned home by the great church of St. Mary Major's, which we entered; and having adored the blessed Sacrament, we venerated a portion of the Crib, which is enclosed in a superb reliquary over its own special altar, and which had been presented to the church by Pius IX., at a cost of twenty-five thousand scudi. We arranged with one of the canons to say mass here on the following morning—a very great and consoling privilege.

V.

ST. MARY MAJOR'S.

The traditions of the Church tell us St. Mary Major's owes its foundation to a miracle—the *miracle of the snow.*

In the beginning of the sixth century there lived in Rome a patrician named John Childless, he and his virtuous spouse resolved to consecrate their wealth to God.

Having prayed to know the divine will, heaven favored them with a vision.

The blessed Virgin appeared to them. "You shall build," said she, "in my honor, a basilica upon the hill of Rome which to-morrow shall be covered with snow."

The same night, she appeared to Pope Liberius and commanded him to erect a church on that part of the Esquiline hill which he should find covered with snow; adding that he should be assisted by the patrician—John. It was the night of the 4th of August, when the heat in Italy is greatest.

The next morning the Esquiline was covered with snow. The whole city rushed to see the miracle. John having beheld it, repaired to the Lateran, to make known to the Pontiff the vision he had had.

The Pope immediately repaired to the spot, the cause of the prodigy was made known ; the church was soon built at the expense of the saintly patrician and his spouse.

St. Mary Major's, also called the Liberian Basilica, is the third in rank of the great churches of Rome. The interior is surpassingly beautiful. There are three naves, divided by 44 Ionic columns in white marble, supposed to have been taken from the temple of Juno Licina. The roof is flat, and divided into five rows of panels. It is elaborately carved, and gilt with the first gold brought to Spain from South America, presented to Alexander VI. by Ferdinand and Isabella. Over the high altar rises the baldacchino erected by Benedict XIV. from designs of *Fuga* : it is supported by four Corinthian columns of red porphyry, entwined with gilt bronze palm-leaves, and surmounted by four angels in marble.

The Sixtine and Borghese chapels are indescribable: the latter cost £400,000 sterling—about two millions of dollars.

The miraculous painting of the Virgin and Child, the same which St. Gregory the Great carried in procession to stay the plague that desolated Rome in A. D. 590, is here most religiously preserved.

On the festival of the Assumption, His Holiness assists here at mass, and afterwards gives his benediction, *Urbi et Orbi*, from the balcony over the grand entrance to the church.

C

VI.

ST. PAUL'S ON THE OSTIAN WAY.

A mile and a quarter outside the Porta San Paolo, stands the *Basilica Ostiensis*—a temple not unworthy of the Apostle of the Gentiles.

It was commenced by the Emperors Valentinian II. and Theodosius in A. D. 388, on the site of a more ancient basilica founded by Constantine, over the catacomb of Lucina, a Roman lady who had embraced Christianity, and completed by Honorius in 395 ; Leo III. restored it in the eighth century. Hither was removed the body of St. Paul from the Vatican in A. D. 251, inclosed in a stone urn, on which was engraved the name of the Apostle. The body of St. Timothy also rests under the high altar. Here upon a side altar, is seen thé miraculous crucifix that spoke to Saint Bridgit.

The Church of the Tre Fontana—or three fountains—merits a visit. This is the scene of the martyrdom of St. Paul, and three fountains are said to have sprung up, as the sacred head rebounded thrice, after being severed from the body.

The column, inclosed in an iron grating, at which the saint was beheaded, is kept here with great veneration, and no Catholic ever fails to touch it with reverence, or to drink of the waters of the holy fountains. On this road—Via Ostia—a small chapel marks the place of separation of Sts. Peter and Paul, on their way to suffer death. The inscription runs thus :—" *In questo luogo Si Separa-*

rono S. Pietro e S. Paolo andando al martirio ; e dice Paolo a Pietro : la pace sia teco fondamento della chiesa e pastore di tutti gli agnelli di christo.—E Pietro a Paolo : Va in pace predicatore dei buoni e guida della salute dei giusti."

" At this place St. Peter and St. Paul on their way to suffer martyrdom, separated; and Paul said to Peter: May peace be with thee, foundation of the Church and Pastor of all the lambs of Christ. And Peter said to Paul: Go in peace, thou preacher of the good, and guide of the just, in the way of salvation."

There are three churches hard by, within very little distance of each other. One is called Scala Cœli—the ladder of heaven—and within its vaults lie the remains of St. Zeno, and his twelve thousand companions.

Some fine mosaics recently found at Ostia are to be seen in this interesting place, which has lately been entrusted by the Sovereign Pontiff to the Trappist monks, who are planting the Eucalyptus, and endeavoring to drain the adjacent territory and render the locality more healthy.

The Abbot pointed out to us an ancient road lately discovered, which leads to a temple of Diana, about a mile and a-half distant. It was getting late, so we had to forego the pleasure of visiting it. It was a beautiful evening, and as we drove back to the city we enjoyed the glorious Italian sunset, casting its golden rays upon the Alban hills, and lighting up the pretty villages that grace their lordly sides.

CHAPTER IV.

THE best preserved of all the ancient buildings of Rome, and the one that retains more than any other its original appearance, is the Pantheon. It was the grandest of the many monuments that studded the immense plain of the Campus Martius.

As the name indicates, this temple in pagan times was dedicated to all the Gods. It is a rotunda, and lies between the Corso and the Piazza Navona.

It was built in honor of Jupiter Avenger—in the year 27, before Christ, by Agrippa; and afterwards restored by Septimus Severus and Caracalla, in the year 202 of the Christian era. The interior is 142 feet in diameter; the vast structure receives all its light from a circular opening in the roof. Boniface IV. converted this precious monument to Christian uses, consecrating it to the only true God, under the invocation of the blessed Virgin and the holy martyrs; hence its name at present—*Santa Maria ad Martyres.*

He transported hither from the catacombs twenty-eight chariot loads of the sacred remains of the martyrs, and placed in it an antique image of the Madonna which the chapter of Saint Peter's crowned in 1652, with a diadem of gold.

Fifteen recesses practiced in the walls which are twenty-five feet in thickness, serve admirably for altars. Behind the third one on the left rest the remains of the immortal

Raphael. Here, too, is kept the heart of the great and good Cardinal Consalvi, the faithful minister of Pius VII.

The baths of Agrippa adjoined the Pantheon. Indeed it is thought that this temple was only a portion, one of the halls, of this immense edifice.

From the Pantheon I went to visit the Church of San Andrea della Fratti, rendered famous by the apparition of the blessed Virgin, in 1842, to the Jew Ratisbonne, who immediately became a Christian,—became a priest and ended by going to Jerusalem to labor there for the conversion of his unhappy countrymen.

The grand altar of this church is composed of precious marbles and bronze richly gilt. Its cost was eighty thousand scudi—quite enough to build a splendid church anywhere else.

Leaving, we went on to "La Trinita di Monti," overlooking that very fashionable quarter the "Piazza d'Espagna." The "Trinita" was built by Charles VII. King of France, and now contains one of the finest frescoes extant—the descent from the cross—by Volterra.

This noble church at present belongs to the ladies of the Sacred Heart; their convent and academy adjoin it. It is here, painted on the wall of a vast corridor, that is to be seen the lovely picture called *Mater Admirabilis*. This spot has been converted into a chapel, and since the visit of the Pope in 1846, when he came to pray before it, has been renowned far and wide, and become a sort of pilgrimage. Catholics from all parts of the world love to visit this venerable shrine, to invoke her who never fails those who seek her aid.

Many beautiful *ex votos* have been offered here in gratitude for favors obtained. Through the kindness of one of the nuns, we were favored with some of the oil from the lamps ever burning before this miraculous image.

Before returning from our lengthy promenade we entered the Church of St. Mary of Egypt, and venorated another miraculous picture of the Madonna.

The church stands on the site—probably on the very foundation—of the temple of *Fortuna Virilis*, which is said to have been built by Servius Tullius, sixth King of Rome.

Saint Pius V. gave this church to the Ambassador of the King of Armenia, for the use of the people of that nation. It boasts of a very exact model of the "Holy Sepulchre." This afternoon we had also the pleasure of visiting the "Capitol," and its magnificent museums, containing a mine of wealth in statues, painting, bronzes and inscriptions. Here we feasted our eyes upon that masterpiece, "The Dying Gladiator," so beautifully described by Byron in his "Childe Harold," and which Bell, a true critic, declares "a most tragical and touching representation, upon which no one can meditate without the most melancholy feelings."

> "I see before me the gladiator lie:
> He leans upon his hand—his manly brow
> Consents to death, but conquers agony,
> And his droop'd head sinks gradually low—
> And through his side the last drops, ebbing slow
> From the red gash, fall heavy, one by one,
> Like the first of a thunder shower; and now
> The arena swims around him—he is gone,
> Ere ceased the inhuman shout which hail'd the wretch who won

> He heard it, but he heeded not—his eyes
> Were with his heart, and that was far away ;
> He reck'd not of the life he lost, nor prize,
> But where his rude hut by the Danube lay,
> There were his young barbarians all at play,
> There was their Dacian mother--he, their sire,
> Butcher'd to make a Roman holiday.
> All this rush'd with his blood, shall he expire,
> And unavenged ? Arise, ye Goths, and glut your ire ! "
>
> —BYRON.

The Etruscan statue, a young man picking a thorn from his foot, is to the life, and alone well repays a visit to the Capitoline hill, formerly called *Mons Saturninus*, The great church of *Ara Cœli* stands on the left and is reached by a grand staircase, composed of one hundred and twenty-four steps taken from ancient buildings, and principally, it is said, from the temple of Quirinus.

In the Ara Cœli, during Christmas-tide, a splendid Creche attracts admiring thousands, who piously venerate the image carved in wood from the garden of Olives, of the *Santissimo Bambino* (the Most Holy Child), by a Monk of St. Francis.

At the foot of the Capitol we come upon the Mamertine prison built, according to Titus Livy, by Ancus Martius, fourth King of Rome, 630 years before Christ.

" In this desolate, dark, infectious and terrible place, as Sallust calls it, Jugurtha, King of Numidia, died of hunger, the accomplices of Catiline were strangled by order of Cicero, and at various times a host of others."

The great interest for the Christian is, that within these gloomy walls St. Peter and St. Paul were imprisoned eight or nine months.

We drank of the waters of the miraculous well, which the prince of the Apostles caused to spring, that he might baptise the guards, Processus and Martinien, and the prisoners who declared themselves Christians. Immediately over the Mamertine prison is built the Church of St. Peter in Carcere, famous for its crucifix, and above this, another dedicated to St. Joseph, and belonging to the confraternity of carpenters. In the prison is shown the column to which the apostle was chained.

As we issue forth we enter upon the Forum, and have before us the grand old arch of Septimus Severus, erected in A.D. 205, by the senate and people in honor of the Emperor and his sons Caracalla and Geta, in memory of their victory over the Parthians and Persians. It is of white marble, and consists of a central and two side arches.

We finished this most interesting afternoon by inspecting the *Cloaca Maxima*, that has drained the eternal city for twenty-four centuries, constructed by Tarquin the elder, a portion of which still exists in a state of excellent preservation, not wanting a single stone. Near by is the Church of St. George in Velabro, and the arch of Janus Quadrifons. Saw the spot were Romulas and Remus are said to have been exposed.

CHAPTER V.

BASILICA OF SAINT JOHN OF LATERAN.

THIS celebrated Basilica derives its name from the Senator Plautinus Lateranus, and occupies the very site of his house.

Tacitus mentions him as having been implicated in the conspiracy of Piso. His property was confiscated and he was put to death by Nero.

In the fourth century. Constantine the Great gave the Lateran house to the Bishop of Rome for his residence. An inscription on each side of the grand entrance styles it:—"*Omnium Urbis et Orbis Ecclesiarum Mater et Caput.*" "The Mother and Head of all the Churches of the City and of the World."

St. Sylvester invested it with the the title of the Episcopal Church of the Roman Pontiffs.

The chapter of the Lateran still takes precedence of that of St. Peter's. The ceremony of taking possession of the Lateran Basilica is one of the first observed on the election of a new pope, whose coronation takes place in it, so that for fifteen hundred years it has preserved its rank and privileges.

The great front is a fine specimen of the architecture of the last century : it is built entirely of travertine, consisting of four large columns and six pilasters of the composite order, sustaining a massive entablature and balustrade, surmounted by colossal statues of our Saviour and the saints. Between the columns and pilasters are fine balconies; from that in the centre the Pope gives his benediction to the people on Ascension Thursday.

Over the grand altar, in which is contained a table of wood upon which St. Peter is said to have offered the holy sacrifice, in splendid reliquaries, are preserved the heads of St. Peter and St. Paul, and high up in the Chapel of the Blessed Sacrament, encased in gilt bronze, is the table of cedar wood at which our Lord ate the last Supper with His apostles.

At a little distance from the Basilica is the baptisterium, an octagonal building. Here Constantine received baptism from the hands of St. Sylvester.

In the interior are two massive doors of bronze taken from the baths of Caracalla, which emit a most musical sound on being closed. Many beautiful mosaics of the fifth and seventh centuries adorn this historical place.

The Lateran palace stands near the great Basilica; it is a noble building. It is rich in paintings, statues, frescoes, and a fine collection in terra cotta representing American Indians, admirably executed.

Along its vast corridors are ranged many beautifully preserved sarcophagi taken from the vestibules of the early churches and catacombs, things of vast antiquity.

The bas-reliefs on these generally represent the "Good Shepherd," "Jonas," "Adam and Eve," "The Nativity," "The Resurrection," "the Restoring Light to the Blind," "The Widow of Naim," and other scriptural subjects.

The Lateran cloisters are very beautiful, designed in

the gothic style of the thirteenth, or as some affirm, the twelfth century.

The episcopal throne of Saint Sylvester is still to be seen here; columns from Pilate's house, one split in its whole length, from top to bottom, rent like the rocks on Good Friday; the porphyry slab on which the soldiers cast lots for the seamless garment; another supported on four pillars, six feet high, thought to be the exact stature of our Lord, and many other interesting objects from the holy city, the scene of the Redeemer's passion and death.

During our visit, some Yankee ladies, finding that we spoke English, began to put us through our catechism, as to the authenticity of the monuments here exhibited.

Hailing from the land of wooden hams and wooden nutmegs, evidently they would fain make others believe their country was not alone in imposition. However, when some of our party reminded them how scrupulously those objects were cherished, and that—if exhibited to those anxious to see them—it was always gratuitously, without the hope of a fee, and not as in Westminster Abbey, St. Paul's, and other similar places, where one must always have his sixpence ready, they thought " there was something in that," and if they did not admit everything was genuine yet concluded that those who guard these things with such religious care are not likely to be imposters.

To-day (27th December), quite cold; hailing in the morning. Third Session of the Council at St. Peter's—His Grace, the Archbishop of Baltimore—Dr. Spalding, celebrated the mass. Seven bishops addressed the august assembly.

CHAPTER VI.

MY DIARY.

JANUARY 1st, 1870.—Delightful day : cool, but very fine, reminding us of our lovely October weather at home. Last evening with Father O'Reilly visited the monastery of the Santi Apostoli, to see the beautiful Christmas-crib: —not equal to that of the Franciscans, at the Ara-Cœli.

In this church, dei Santi Apostoli, lie the remains of Clement XIV., a member of this monastery before his elevation to the throne of St. Peter. Michael Angelo died in this parish, March, 1614. Here his body reposed before being removed to Florence.

Leaving the monastery, we hastened to the "Gesu" to see the arrival of the Pope, who came to assist at the Benediction and Te Deum, in thanksgiving to God for the mercies of the year. His Holiness came in *demi-gala*, still the turn-out was very grand, and the enthusiasm of the multitude unbounded. As he drove up to the piazza, cheer upon cheer rent the air. The great church was densely crowded : thousands knelt outside to receive the blessing of the Vicar of Christ.

To-day a papal chapel was held at St. Peter's : a great many bishops were present, and as usual an immense concourse of the faithful. The day—New Year's—was cold, but fine. Early in the morning I perceived a little ice in a shaded spot, on the street. In the evening we dined with Mr. O'Brien of New Orleans, at the "Minerva," and met His Lordship of Galveston, Texas; and the venerable Curé of the cathedral of New Orleans, who had just been named by the Pope—Prothonotary Apostolic.

JANUARY 5th.—Cold, but fine clear day. After dinner drove out by the Porta di San Pancrazio, and to San Pietro in Montorio. Here Pius IX. intended placing the monumental column of the Vatican Council. This fine church, occupying one of the finest sites in Rome, was the late Cardinal Cullen's title. It stands upon the spot occupied by the Arx Janiculensis, of Ancus Martius, and derives its name from the golden sand of which the hill is composed.

The immortal Pius, in giving its first Cardinal to the martyr-nation, rendered the honor doubly precious by giving to his Eminence a temple dear to every Irish heart, as containing the ashes of Hugh O'Neil, son of the Earl of Tyrone, and of Roderick O'Donnell, Earl of Tyrconnell, who died in the eternal city, early in the 17th century.

From Montorio is had the best view of Rome and the outlying country, from Soracte to the ends of the Alban hills, studded with their pretty villages and towns. Returning home, we passed a small enclosure with a monument erected by the Pope, to mark the place where the head of the apostle St. Andrew, stolen during the revolution, was fortunately recovered,

To-night our rooms are quite cosy; we have fire for the

first time—and we almost fancy ourselves in Canada—
" the dearest spot on earth to me." Some of our clerical
friends have much grander apartments; but none of
them are really as comfortable as we. Monseigneur thinks
of everything but himself.

JANUARY 6th.—After my mass, celebrated in the room
in which lived for some time, St. Catharine of Sienna,
there being a *function*, I drove over to St. Peter's. The
Pope was present at the throne and received the obedience of the Cardinals. His Holiness looked well, and
his fine, clear, sonorous voice was remarked by all.

I left before the ceremony was over and with some
friends visited some of the neighboring churches.

It was a lovely morning. We ascended the hill to St.
Onuphrio, from which we had an enchanting view of the
city.

In this church is the tomb of Tasso, and over it his
portrait. A splendid mausoleum is being erected to his
memory by Pius IX., who seems, in his fatherly care, to
forget nothing.

Attached to San Onuphrio are two cemeteries, beautifully kept; in one the " Holy Way of the Cross " is frescoed
upon the walls. Dark cypress trees shade this hallowed
place, so worthy of the dead.

In the afternoon I went to hear one of the French
bishops preach at San Andrea della Valle. The audience
was large; the sermon very much appreciated. The

French clergy, as a rule, are distinguished for rare eloquence. Over the grand altar of this church, which has one of the most perfect of domes, there is during the Christmas feasts a life-size representation of the adoration of the wise men.

JANUARY 8th.—This morning was held another Session of the Council. Heard the Archbishop of Baltimore preach this afternoon. Subject—" Conversion of the Nations." Speaking of the bishops assembled, he said : One had travelled 21,000 miles, in obedience to the voice of the Vicar of Christ.

JANUARY 11th.—Being very fine, after dinner I drove with His Lordship—Mgr. Horan to the beautiful Church of Santa Agnese, fuori le mura (outside the walls).

Under the Confession lie the bodies of St. Agnes and of her foster sister, St. Emerentiana.

Hard by, we also visited the church built by Constantine, in the year 324, over the place where the body of this sweet little saint was found.

It is a rotunda, giving one an excellent idea of the churches of the fourth century. It possesses some of the rarest mosaics. There is also the splendid bust of our Lord in white marble, the work of Michael Angelo.

In 1854, Pius IX. visited the Convent and Church of St. Agnes. A vast crowd greeted His Holiness. The floors of this hall in which they were assembled gave way —yet no one was injured seriously—a truly miraculous escape. The 12th of April, anniversary of this accident, and which corresponds with the date of the Pope's return from Gaeta, is celebrated with great solemnity. In thanksgiving to God for his escape, Pius IX. ordered the restoration of the Basilica at his own expense.

To-day, for the first time, I visited the catacombs, and saw in many of the *loculi* skulls, a vial filled with martyr's blood; and other relics of the early church. We were honored in the evening with a visit from my Lord of Hamilton, the good, the amiable Bishop Farrell—"beloved of God and men." Alas! that he was not spared longer to the Church of Canada.

JANUARY 12th.—Pleasant day; drove out on the Appian road to San Sebastiano. Under the altar reposes the body of this saint.

In a side chapel, also beneath an altar, is a splendid life-size statue, recumbent, of this glorious confessor of the faith, whose name the late Cardinal Wiseman has rendered so familiar in his exquisite work—" Fabiola."

We descended into the catacombs and saw the place where Saint Cecilia's body had been laid, and the resting-places of Saints Tiburtius and Valerianus.

Here, too, were pointed out to us the Sarcophagus of St.

Stephen, pope and martyr; and the chapel, or cubiculum, with the altar, at which he offered the holy Sacrifice; on the tabernacle are figures of the child Jesus and two lovely little boy angels. Elsewhere they showed us the marble cross formerly placed above the Pontiff's chair.

On the Appian way is met the little church of the "Domine, quo vadis."

An ancient tradition relates that St. Peter, fleeing by night from the persecution of Nero, met near this place his Divine Master.

"Whither goest thou, O Lord"—exclaimed the apostle. Jesus answered him, "I am going to Rome, to be crucified again." St. Peter understood the reproach; returned to the city, and soon after sealed his love and his faith with his life's blood. Farther on, about two miles from the Porta di San Sebastiano, is the famous tomb of Cecilia Metella, erected to her upwards of nineteen centuries ago.

It resembles a martello tower; and such is its solidity, that in the 13th century, the Caetanis used it as a fortress Lord Byron in his "Childe Harold" has thrown a halo around this venerable tomb, that lends to it an additional interest, for all the lovers of his immortal lays:

> There is a stern round tower of other days
> Firm as a fortress, with its fence of stone,
> Such as an army's baffled strength delays,
> Standing with half its battlements alone,
> And with two thousand years of ivy grown,
> The garland of eternity, where wave
> The green leaves over all by time o'erthrown;—
> What was this tower of strength? within its cave
> What treasure lay so lock'd, so hid?—A woman's grave."
> —BYRON.

JANUARY 14th.—To-day we strayed among the ruins of the baths of Caracalla, and near by in a vineyard examined the remains of a beautiful house, lately discovered far beneath the surface.

Many rooms, as well as the atrium, are well preserved. The coloring of the walls and the frescoes seem as if executed but a few years ago.

Collected within this vineyard are marbles, portions of statues, busts, amphoræ, lamps, vases and numerous other vestiges of days gone by.

Another session of the Vatican Council was held this morning at St. Peter's.

Letters from Canada! how welcome!

On the invitation of Monsignor Kirby, we dined at the Irish College, with His Eminence Cardinal Cullen, and several Australian and Irish bishops.

JANUARY 14th.—This morning, Bishop McGill, of Richmond, Virginia, preached at San Andrea della Valle.

In the afternoon, at the same place, I had the pleasure of hearing the celebrated Mgr. Pie, of Poictiers, who delivered a most telling discourse upon the infallibility of the Pope; proving from the writings of St. Hilary, formerly Bishop of the same See, that even in the days of that great saint the Catholic world believed that the Roman Pontiff, in faith and morals, teaching as Head of the Church, was divinely preserved from error. Mgr. Pie, later on, was created a Cardinal, by Pius IX.

Here also, Bishop Ullathorne, of Birmingham, preached. The sermon I relished above all others was that of His Grace the Archbishop of Westminster.

For an hour and fifteen minutes he held his audience spell-bound, while he spoke on the "Unity of the Church."

The Doctor, now Cardinal Manning, is a man of most intellectual, ascetic, appearance. Everything is in his favor; his manner, his gestures, his voice, his saintly look. The vast audience was enraptured with his masterly discourse. Announcing at the close of his sermon a collection for the propagation of the faith, he paid a beautiful tribute to the piety of dear old long-suffering Ireland, and to that other generous, noble nation—her sister—fair Catholic France.

JANUARY 17th.—This afternoon the students of the Propaganda gave their celebrated polyglot séance, at which addresses were delivered in thirty different languages. Cardinal Barnabo presided; great many foreigners present. A negro from Senegambia, and but lately ordained priest, spoke and apparently very eloquently. At the close of the session, five little fellows returned thanks in verse in five languages; and roars of laughter greeted the last who concluded his rhyme with,—" And as a certain great nation would say, Arrah! may your shadows never grow less."

The College of the Propaganda was founded in 1622 by Gregory XV., for the purpose of educating as missionaries young foreigners from infidel or heretical countries, who might afterwards return and spread the Catholic faith among their countrymen. Urban VIII. erected the present building. The library contains upwards of 30,000 volumes. A printing office, rich in Oriental types, is attached to the Propaganda. Over two hundred students receive their education gratis,—everything being supplied to them in this world-renowned institution. The diocese of Kingston once counted among its priests several who had studied within these classic halls: Dr. Chisholm, Drs. Patrick and John Madden, and others.

JANUARY 19th.—This morning, being the festival of the Chair of St. Peter, I went to the great Basilica, and being fortunate enough to secure a place near the "Confession," saw to great advantage the ceremonies of the day.

His Holiness was present at the throne, and entered and left the church in the "Sede Gestatoria." As usual, there was an immense throng; many cardinals and bishops assisted at the functions.

We spent the afternoon among the splendid paintings of the Colonna palace, one of the finest in Rome. The picture gallery is open every day except Sunday. Three halls decorated with most precious tapestries are met before entering those devoted to the paintings.

JANUARY 20th.—To-day we visited the Vatican library and the great paintings. The collection is small, but the most valuable in the world.

The "Last Communion of Jerome," and the "Transfiguration," by Raphael, are here—the only place on earth worthy of them. The former is acknowledged as Domenichino's masterpiece, and the glory of the Bolognese school.

The latter is the last and greatest effort of the "divine Raphael," and alone would immortalize him.

The Vatican library, counting the galleries opening from it, is twelve hundred feet in length.

A charming visit was also made to the splendid collection of Prince Borghese, comprising 800 pictures, distributed in twelve halls.

The Roman nobility kindly throw open their magnificent halls to the public. Here were many young artists, male and female, copying the lovely pictures.

A fine drive on the Appian road, for about five miles, filled up the afternoon. Besides other interesting sights was that of the baths of Caracalla.

During our drive we saw much of the Campagna, and of the immense ruins of the ancient aqueducts. The distant mountains were capped with snow, and the gorgeous sunset in a cloudless heaven, lent additional beauty to the scene. Though far away, we could see distinctly the quaint old towns of Frascati, Monte Rotondo, Montona—celebrated by the bravery of the Papal Zouaves—and Rocca di Papa. On our way we met the celebrated Bishop of Orleans, Mgr. Dupanloup, and Mgr. Maret, both just then much spoken of as Inopportunists.

Being the festival of Sts. Fabian and Sebastian, we visited their church and venerated their relics. The head of the former is kept in a silver and crystal case. We descended into the catacombs of this church and saw the place where the bodies of St. Peter and St. Paul were first entombed.

JANUARY 21st.—At St. Agnes'—outside the walls—for the ceremony of the blessing of the lambs, the wool of which is afterwards spun by nuns and made into Palliums destined for archbishops.

The ceremony, new of course to us, was interesting. His Eminence Cardinal Barrili officiated, and in the sanctuary, besides the mitred Abbot of the monastery, there were six priests in chasubles and eight wearing dalmatics.

The lambs were carried in on silver dishes, after the mass, and placed upon the altar. An occasional bleating was heard, causing much merriment among the lookers on. The music was excellent. I assisted at vespers in another church on the Piazza Navona, dedicated to the saint, and which stands upon the very site of her martyrdom.

The office was pontifical; the singing superb and evidently much appreciated by the large and very fashionable assemblage, principally foreigners.

In the basement of this church is shown the *locum turpitudinis* where the young saint was exposed and where she was visibly protected by an angel. The inscription runs thus :—"*Ingressa Agnes turpitudinis locum angelum Domini præparatum invenit.*" A bas-relief over the altar represents the saint miraculously covered by her hair.

JANUARY 23rd.—To-day His Eminence Cardinal de Bonnechose, Monsignor Fessler, Secretary of the Council, and other dignitaries dined at the French Seminary, where we boarded. Of course we *had all de sumptuosities ob de season.* The Cardinal, now dead, was tall, distinguished-looking, and rather handsome. The Mgr. could lay claim to none of these, but no doubt was a clever man to be selected for such an important rôle by the Pontiff.

His Eminence had been a lawyer in France, and a Huguenot, as Protestants are termed there.

Yesterday, though disagreeable, wet and cold, did not prevent my usual promenade. With Bishop Grimley, of Cape Town, South Africa, a most saintly man, since gone to his reward. and his Secretary, Father O'Reilly, author of the "Martyrs of the Coliseum," etc., I paid a most interesting visit to San Pietro in Vincoli, a grand basilica situated on the northern part of the Esquiline Hill. Here we venerated the very chains with which St. Peter had been bound, and assisted at Benediction of the Blessed Sacrament, at which a Cardinal officiated.

This church was built in the year 442, by Eudoxia, wife

of the Emperor Valentinian III. "There is seen the MOSES of *Michael Angelo,* one of the most celebrated productions of his gigantic genius."

Here Popes John II., in 532, and St. Gregory, in 1073, were elected to the Sovereign Pontificate. The street before this church is supposed to correspond with the *Vicus-Sceleratus,* through which Tullia drove her car over the dead body of her father.

The Papal choir was present at Benediction, and sang one of the most exquisite litanies ever composed.

We spent a pleasant evening at Madam M———'s, meeting a very select company, among which was the Archbishop of Calcutta, several bishops from Ireland, and other persons of note.

JANUARY 24th.—This morning to San Augustino. This church was built by William—Guillaume d'Estouteville, Archbishop of Rouen, Cardinal under Eugene IV., and Dean of the Sacred College. The cupola was the first raised at Rome; it dates from 1580. The frescoes, paintings, marbles and gildings are very fine. The church is much frequented by women in delicate health, who come to pray before the miraculous statue of the Madonna, who here, as elsewhere, seems never to be invoked in vain.

In the monastary adjoining this church is the *Bibliotheca Angelica,* so named from Cardinal Angelo Rocca, who founded it in 1605.

It is the third most important in Rome; it possesses

90,000 printed works, and 3,000 manuscripts, many of which are Chinese, Syrian and Coptic.

In the afternoon I went again to St. Peter's, spending hours among its wonders, and taking in the "Pieta di Michael Angelo;" the great mosaic of San Sebastiano; the splendid statue of Innocent XII.; the superb tombs of Gregory XIII. and of the two Alexanders—VII. and VIII., with their indescribable bas-reliefs; the meeting of Attila by Pope Leo; the crucifixion of the Prince of the Apostles; the apparition of our Lord to St. Thomas, and many other noble creations that could be inspired only by religion, and that—divine. Beneath the altar surmounted by the gorgeous mosaic of the death of St. Peter, repose the bodies of Sts. Simon and Jude. Another great mosaic is that where the apostle is represented raising Tabitha to life.

The tombs of Pius VII. and Pius VIII. excite universal admiration—and then we come upon another enchanting mosaic, bright in its coloring as the plumage of some tropical bird, almost a perfect copy of Rome and the world's greatest conception—the "Transfiguration" —the last and greatest of the works of the great master, Raphael, cut off in the prime of life, at the early age of thirty-seven. *Explevit tempora multa!*

This afternoon the Pope came to the Séminaire-Français, to visit the illustrious Bishop of Nimes, Monseigneur Plantier, who had by his vigorous writings ably defended the doctrine of the infallibility—and who was then dangerously ill. His Holiness remained with the good bishop about quarter of an hour, and afterward, in the grand Salon of the Seminary, admitted the community and the priests—their guests—to the kissing of his feet.

His Holiness charmed all by his kind manner and affability, having a little gracious word for each one presented to him. Unfortunately I was, as usual, off visiting the churches and other monuments, and thus missed the papal audience.

JANUARY 27th.—Called to-day at the Irish College, and returning went into the "Gesu"—the principal church of the Jesuits in Rome.

Here, above the altar of Saint Ignatius, is the largest and finest piece of *lapis-lazuli*, known; a most costly marble.—It is in the form of a globe, and supports the solid silver statue of the saint, of fabulous price.

Another charming drive out to the great St. Paul's, which one never tires of visiting. Vespers were going on; a large number of strangers was present: the music was very good. The portraits of all the Roman Pontiffs —in gorgeous mosaics—from St. Peter, adorn the upper part of the interior of this magnificent basilica, beyond doubt, interiorly, the second grandest in Rome.

JANUARY 29th.—Walked out with Lieutenant Murray to the famous Ponte Salaro. This bridge was constructed of huge square blocks of red-stone-tufa, and dates back to the oldest Roman period.

In October, 1867, it was blown up by the papal troops in order to prevent the entry of Garibaldi's ruffians.

A little beyond this bridge lies the plain where many bloody encounters took place between the Romans and the Etruscans, under the kings; and particularly that of the Fidenates and Veientes, which resulted in the destruction of Alba-Longa, by Tullius Hostilius, through the treachery of Mettus Fufetius, the leader of the auxilaries from this town.

We passed a farm, now the property of the Irish College, containing the catacombs of Santa Priscilla. Strange to say, here was discovered the body of Saint Celestine, the pope that sent St. Patrick to preach to the Irish nation.

Being not a little fatigued by our very long walk, we refreshed ourselves at a little way side Osteria, where we got some light, but delicious wine, and for almost nothing How often, when abroad, have we regretted the want of some such harmless drink for our people.

In France and Italy no one is ever—scarcely ever—seen intoxicated. The wine often is generous enough to send a pleasant glow through the veins, and even warm the countenance; but one does not see the blear eyes, the red red nose, the purple streaks, like clotted gore, that but too plainly tell the depth and frequency of the potations of many people in our own country and clearly indicate the "valitudinarian debauchee." The urchin that waited on us had a sore head, and vividly recalled to my mind Dr. Johnson's story of the pudding in the Highland inn.

Before drinking, however, we rinsed our glasses,—the lad apparently wondering at such fastidiousness.

This was my longest walk—about six miles—since I came to Rome. We drove a great deal, and Monseigneur insists on always paying for the carriage. This he claims as his privilege—and of course one must yield. His heart was certainly in the right place.

JANUARY 31st.—Saw His Holiness as he passed in his carriage; knelt and received his benediction. He honored the American College to-day with a visit, and granted an audience to the bishops, clergy and students. This morning I paid a visit to Mgr. MacEvilly, of Galway, now Archbishop of Tuam, successor to the late John McHale —O'Connell's "Lion of Judah."

While in Rome I frequently met their lordships, the Bishops of Limerick, Galway, and the coadjutor of Killaloe—amiable and saintly Dr. Power. With them I was always a welcome guest, and most warmly and graciously received; and when leaving Rome, their lordships gave me the most flattering introduction to their respective clergy.

Since returning to Canada I had the honor to receive a letter of thanks from His Grace of Tuam, acknowledging the cheque for one hundred pounds sterling, sent to him by me, for his suffering people.

This was one of the many noble contributions of the generous and pious Catholics of St. Francis Xavier's, Brockville, ever ready and willing to correspond with every appeal of their pastor. God be with them!

A goodly part of the afternoon was devoted to San Clemente. We went to venerate the relics of St. Ignatius of Antioch—it being his feast; and to hear the great Dominican, Father Tom Burke, who was to pronounce the panegyric of the saint.

The eloquent preacher always attracted large and distinguished audiences. To-day he almost surpassed himself; his discourse was listened to with unspeakable delight by the vast concourse assembled, English-speaking, of course.

Leaving this ancient basilica, built by Paschal II. in 1099-1118, I again entered the Coliseum, and, kneeling at the cross planted in the centre, prayed fervently to God and the glorious martyr who, in this very place, 1760 years before, had died—torn to pieces by wild beasts—for the faith of the One, holy, Catholic and Apostolic Church.

(The subjoined are from the Bishops of Limerick and Galway :

"*Cum Rev. D. Isaac Joannes MacCarthy sit dignissimus Sacerdos celebret in Diœcesi. Galvieni, &. &.—Eum clero nostro maximopere commendamus.*"

† JOANNES EPIS. GALVIENSIS ETE.

Rome—Die 25 Aprilis, 1870.

"*Celebret in Diœcesi Limericensi, cujus clero eum vehementer commendamus.*"

† GEORGIUS BUTLER.
Epis. Limericensis.

Datum Romæ, Die 25 Aprilis, 1870.

What enhances the great kindness of these distinguished prelates is, these letters were not solicited—

needless to say these documents are still preserved and dearly cherished by the recipient.

FEBRUARY 2nd.—Festival of the Purification of the Blessed Virgin Mary—Candlemas day.

His Lordship and I reached St. Peter's just in time to see the entry of the Pope, who was carried in the "Sede-Gestatoria."

After blessing the candles, His Holiness distributed them to the cardinals, bishops, royal personages and to the members of the diplomatic corps.

The procession then moved through the great church, Pius IX. being again borne on his throne, holding a lighted taper in his hand, and fervently praying as he passed along.

He wore a Roman purple cope and the white mitre.

On our return home, Mgr., with his usual kindness, gave me the large waxen candle presented to him at the ceremony by the Sovereign Pontiff.

I still cherish this precious souvenir; it is much shorter than originally—pieces of it having been given to pious friends. His Lordship of Galway gave me a little work to-day on devotion to St. Joseph, my great protector.

The Cardinal Archbishop of Bordeaux and several strange bishops dined at the French Seminary; it was a grand affair.

February 3rd.—This morning, in company with the Rev. Abbé Simonis, of Alsace, and his young friend, we left for Tivoli, the ancient Tibur, a city of the Sicarri, which was founded nearly five centuries before Rome, whose rival it was, until reduced to obedience by Camillus.

We were favored with beautiful weather; my companions were most charming men—wonderfully entertaining.

We spent a delightful day visiting the curiosities of this ancient town, and many objects of interest that render Tivoli so attractive.

We climbed the hills hundreds of feet, with little donkeys, most sure-footed beasts, and gazed with wondering admiration upon the lovely scenery. The cascatelli or falls, the mountain peaks, the deep valleys, the world of charms of this almost enchanted place. In the distance we could see the dome, "the vast and wondrous dome," of St. Peter's standing out in all its magnitude and beauty against the evening sky.

At the Locanda della Sibilli we had a capital dinner, with abundance of excellent wine, and all for a trifle.

My Alsatian friends, though like all their countrymen, French to the back-bone, had retained sufficient of the German to prefer the excellent beer which was to be had in this Locanda, not usually the case in those small Italian inns.

We turned our horses towards the city a little after six, and reached Rome about 9 p.m., where my lord was patiently awaiting my return. I entertained Monseigneur until quite late with a description of our visit to this most interesting old town, which he had visited years before.

FEBRUARY 5th.—Sunday, bright, sparkling day. Delightful weather, lovely; beautiful as the middle of June beneath our northern skies.

Another visit to the Pantheon—as already said, the greatest of the great monuments of the Campus Martius; and in the afternoon a drive to the Ponte Molle, two miles from the city.

This famous bridge was first built by the Censor Marcus Æmilius Scaurus. It was on this bridge the envoys of the Allobroges engaged in the Catiline conspiracy were arrested by order of Cicero, 63 before Christ; and from its parapets the body of Maxentius was thrown into the Tiber, after being defeated by Constantine five miles further up on the Flaminian way:—Via Flaminia.

The present bridge, anciently called *Pons Milvius* was nearly rebuilt by Pius IX.

On our way home, after a charming outing, we visited the Church of San Pancrazio, erected in the year 272 by Pope St. Felix, in honor of this heroic boy who suffered martyrdom at the age of fourteen. This church is rich in historical souvenirs. Within its walls St. Gregory the Great delivered his twenty-seventh homily on the Gospel of St. John.

Here, Peter of Arragon was crowned by Innocent III.,

and later on here John XXII. received Louis, King of Naples.

The French soldiers devastated this sanctuary in 1798, and again it was polluted by the wretched hordes of the monster Garibaldi, in 1849. During the siege of Rome it was the centre of the operations of the French troops.

In this church was buried Crescentius Nomentatus, the celebrated ruler of Rome in the 10th century. Here also Narses, after having defeated Totila, met the Pope and cardinals, and marched in procession to St. Peter's to return thanks. The remains of St. Pancratius and St. Victor are deposited in the Confession.

FEBRUARY 7th.—Another delightful afternoon at St. Peter's. Months and months might be spent in this magnificent temple and still there would be much to see and to admire. Those who spend but a few weeks in Rome can know and see but little of the wonders of the eternal city.

After adoring the Blessed Sacrament, I told my beads at the tomb of the apostles, praying fervently for the loved ones in my far-off Canadian home.

The last rays of the setting sun cast their golden light through the vast basilica, as I turned to leave it, and the words of the Royal psalmist came vividly to my mind: " Lord, I have loved the glory of thy house, and the place where thy glory dwelleth," words which must have often escaped the dying lips of successive pontiffs, who did so much and spent such vast sums on this glorious temple.

On my promenade, twice I met the carriage of His Holiness, and each time received his benediction. How often, already, he has blessed me! Mgr. Horan dined to-day with Monseigneur de Quimper, a grand old bishop, and Louis Venillot, the distinguished editor of the *Univers* the famous antagonist of Monseigneur Dupanloup, Bishop of Orleans.

Venillot resembled the late George Clerk, of the *True Witness*, more than enough to pass for his brother. Last night a little, very little snow fell, all gone this morning. We spent a very pleasant evening at the palatial residence of Madam M———, who had kindly invited His Lordship and me to a soiree musicale, the performers being all professional, and of a very high order. The drawingroom presented a most brilliant appearance, and the concert proved a great success; the very distinguished audience —lay and clerical—left, enchanted with the delightful entertainment, and the charming hospitality of the noble hostess.

FEBRUARY 8th.—This morning we were honored by a visit from His Grace, Mgr. Baillargeon, and his Vicar-General, now the Cardinal Archbishop of Quebec, and formerly one of our professors in the seminary of the ancient capital. To-day, with Bishop Grimly and his secretary, I visited the Monastery of the Passionists—

their head-quarters in Rome—near St. John's of Lateran, to venerate the Scala Santa, which we ascended on our knees. They are never trodden by man's foot.

The great statues, on either side, are the gift of Pius IX., whose munificent generosity is met with so often. We passed a most pleasant evening at the Minerva, with the Bishops of Limerick, Galway, and Killaloe.

FEBRUARY 9th.—Another summer's day. Strolled by the Piazza d'Espagna to the beautiful grounds of the Académie Imperial Français, from which one has a fine view of Rome and its surroundings. Thence to the Pincio, where a gay crowd had assembled to hear the splendid band of the French Legion, one of the best in the service.

Last evening His Holiness presented our friend, Mgr Lootens, Vicar Apostolic of Idaho, with a handsome cameo ring. Another Session of the Council this morning. To-day on my way home—with another young priest—we met Monseigneur de Quimper driving alone. His lordship stopped the carriage—got out—paid the hackman—and insisted on our taking his place, while he returned to the Seminary on foot.

FEBRUARY 10th.—Visited the Basilica of Santa Croce in Gerusalemme (Holy Cross of Jerusalem), built upon the site of the gardens of Sextus Varius, the father of Heliogabalus.

The Sessorian palace, within the enclosure, was inhabited by the latter emperor; afterward by his successor Alexander Severus, and later by St. Helen, mother of Constantine the Great.

The noble basilica was the work of the latter: it was consecrated by Pope St. Sylvester, restored by Gregory II. in the seventh century, and put in its present state by Benedict XIV. in 1743.

Here we venerated several precious relics: three pieces of the true cross, each about nine inches long, by one-and-a-half wide. The color of the wood is a light brown.

We saw one of the nails used in the crucifixion, some of the thorns of our Saviour's crown, and the title of the cross, the letters being still very distinct.

Quite a large piece of the cross of the "Good Thief," and a finger of St. Thomas are here preserved most religiously. A reliquary belonging to Gregory the Great was also exhibited. Beneath the flooring of one of the chapels, is earth brought from Mount Calvary by the Empress St. Helena; and under the high altar, in a fine basaltic urn, rest the bodies of the martyrs Cesareus and Anastasius.

The immense frescoes on the ceiling are very beautiful. They were executed by Pinturechio in 1470, and are still wonderfully fresh. Here the Pope consecrates the Agnus Dei, on Passion Sunday.

From here we drove to Santa Sabina, on Mount Aventine, which was consecrated by Sixtus III. in the year 440.

It was constituted a station for Ash-Wednesday, by Gregory the Great; hither came the Sovereign Pontiffs to receive the blessed ashes.

The present monastery—Dominican—was once a pontifical palace, and inhabited by many popes. A part of it was given by Honorius III. to St. Dominic, when he gave him the church.

Here sojourned St. Raymond de Pennafort, St. Thomas Aquinas, St. Hyacinth—the light of Poland,—his brother St. Ceslas, St. Pius V., and many other great men, eminent for their learning and sanctity.

We visited the cells, now chapels, of St. Pius and St. Dominic, venerating the miraculous crucifix of the former. This church glories in the possession of Sassoferati's great masterpiece—the Madonna with the child Jesus, who is handing a Rosary to Saint Catharine of Sienna, kneeling before him, while St. Dominic is opposite the Blessed Virgin. This is one of the loveliest paintings I have ever seen. The faces of the saints are angelic; the effect of light and shade upon St. Catharine's, simply marvellous.

In the garden of the monastery is an orange tree planted by St. Dominic 682 years ago—(1870)—and still, like the great religious family he established, bearing fruit. One of the Rev. Fathers graciously presented me with some of its leaves, still in my possession.

When the great Lacordaire restored the Order in France, this tree sent forth a new shoot, which bore fruit the same year.

Here again, from a small tribune on which opens a door of the monastery, we enjoyed a grand view of St. Peter's, the Vatican, and the transtiberine country.

On our way home we passed a couple of ancient temples, now consecrated to religion, and inspected the huge arch of Janus, near the Cloaca Maxima.

On the whole, this was one of the most charming days I have spent in Rome.

Monseigneur Lootens accompanied us to-day. His Lordship is like a young student—a very profound one, it must be admitted—and we are never happier than when he is with us in our drives. His conversational powers are remarkable, and though he has a slight foreign accent, he expresses himself with all the accuracy of our most polished speakers.

FEBRUARY 13th.—A visit to-day to the Quirinal Palace, situated on Monte Cavallo.

This palace is immense—worthy of the Sovereign Pontiffs. Paintings, frescoes, gilding, sculptures, tapestries, thrones in crimson and gold, meet the eye constantly, and in their gorgeousness and profusion seem to vie with each other in splendour. We visited the apartments of the Pope, and the room in which Pius VII. was taken prisoner by the orders of Napoleon. Cardinal Pacca accompanied His Holiness to France. The palace gardens are very extensive, and of course most artistically laid out and kept.

From the Quirinal we crossed to the little church opposite, where the Blessed Sacrament is always exposed—by night as well as day.

Crowds were kneeling in adoration, while from beyond the grate came the sweet voices of the holy nuns reciting the divine office. It reminded me strongly of my humble little church at Williamstown, where our faithful people came in such numbers to the sublime devotion of the "Forty Hours' Prayer."

Further on we visited the Franciscan Church, and San Carlo alle Quatro Fontana, which church and convent occupy just the same space that is covered by one of the columns that support the dome of St. Peter's. Then to St Bernard's and St. Mary's of the Angels—formerly portions of the vast baths of Diocletian.

FEBRUARY 17th.—To-day the Pope went in grand state to open the Exhibition of Christian Art. An immense crowd had assembled, and the cheering, as His Holiness drove up and descended from his carriage, was most enthusiastic. He passed very closely to me. The day was cloudy, but fortunately the rain kept off until the papal cortege had returned to the Vatican and the vast concourse had dispersed.

At dinner I had the honor of reading the "Lecture" in Latin, much to the amusement of Nos Seigneurs the French bishops.

His Lordship Mgr. de Beauvais, Noyon et Senlis, presented me with his portrait; no doubt as a reward for the amusement my foreign accent afforded him.

After leaving Rome I received a charming letter from

this most distinguished prelate, kindly inviting me to visit him at Beauvais, near Paris. Indeed I received many marks of esteem from the French bishops and clergy of the Séminaire Français.

FEBRUARY 18th.—A very interesting visit to-day,—the fine old church of the Capuchins—Santa Maria della Concezione.

As we enter, in the first chapel, on the right is Guido's magnificent painting, "St. Michael crushing the devil beneath his feet."

This is considered one of Rome's best pictures. An English critic calls it the Catholic Apollo. "Like the Belvidere God, he says, the Archangel breathes that dignified vengeance which animates without distorting; while the very devil derives importance from his august adversary, and escapes the laugh which his figure usually provokes."

Cardinal Barberini, brother of Urban VIII., for whom this picture was painted, is buried here before the high altar. His tomb is marked by the simple yet grand inscription on the pavement: "Hic jacet pulvis, cinis, et nihil;" *Here lie dust, ashes, and nothing.*

In the chapel opposite Guido's archangel is seen the "Conversion of St. Paul," one of Pietro da Cortona's best efforts. At the gospel side of the grand altar is the tomb of Prince Alexander Sobieski, son of John III., King of Poland; he died in Rome in 1744.

We visited, beneath the church, the four vaulted chambers, where the monks lie buried.

The bones of the dead are arranged here in a most singular manner, forming garlands, wreaths—decorating, if such could decorate, these ghastly chambers.

Some of the bodies are placed standing, others reclining in niches made among the bones; the accumulation of two centuries. The place of interment being small, when a monk dies he is buried in the oldest grave, and the bones of the last occupant removed here. Those we saw had on the same habit in which they had been buried; to the face of some still cling the hard and shrivelled skin. On the whole it was a hideous sight, and to us seems unworthy of the dead. The earth here was originally brought from Jerusalem. Beneath the altar reposes the body of the Blessed Crispin of Viterbo, a lay brother of the order of Capuchins. He died the 19th of May, 1730, and was beatified by Pius VII., the 7th of September, 1806.

February, 19th.—From a window in the Doria palace on the corso, we had much pleasure watching the carnival festivities. When the great bell of the Capitol had tolled, the Governor of Rome proceeded from the Piazza del Popolo, followed by the Senator or Mayor, in great state. Men on horseback headed the cortege, and immediately after the Senator came a grand empty carriage, and then six superb ones, having emblazoned upon the doors and panels the—*S. P. Q. R.*—the initials of the senatorial and civil authority. *Senatus populus que Romanus.*

Many musicians were mounted, while a much greater number, a splendid band, came on foot.

It was really a fine turnout. The horses racing, riderless, was as exciting as it was novel to us. The strewing of *confetti* from the windows and balconies on the passersby, caused much merriment, and many a hearty laugh at the expense of the poor unfortunates, who were whitened from head to foot. No respect of persons; a distinguished French Abbé was *powdered* from head to foot.

All was taken most good naturedly, not the slightest annoyance being manifested; the more they were pelted the more they enjoyed it. No drunken man was to be seen upon the streets, and the thousands, after the fun was over, dispersed as quietly as on a market-day. The police have very little to do on these occasions. The population behave themselves like a lot of good-natured school-boys. At one of the windows in a palace opposite to us occasionally appeared the venerable Cardinal di Moreno, and some other Spanish bishops and priests, taking the least little peep—*tant-soit-peu*—at the performance, which they seemed to relish immensely.

FEBRUARY 20th. — After dinner Mgr. Horan, Mgr. Lootens and I drove out by the Porta del Popolo, to Ponte

Molle, along the Tiber, in by the Porta Angelica, north of St Peter's, and out again by the Porta Cavallagieri, up to the beautiful fountain, Aquæ Paulinæ; thence to Montorio, where the column commemorative of the Vatican Council is to be erected; returning to the city by the Porta San Pancrazio, making a most delightful and instructive afternoon. In the evening I attended a dramatic performance in the Collegio Nazarino, situated near the Fontana di Trevi. It was all Italian, and hence to me unintelligible. Still I much enjoyed the fine music, the rich costumes, the splendid scenery, and, apparently, the very elegant acting. The audience seemed very much pleased. I have never seen anything so well produced in an educational establishment; one might easily have imagined himself in a first-class opera house. This college was founded in 1622, by Cardinal Michael Angelo Conti de Rimini. It is chiefly frequented by the children of the Roman nobility and gentry, and is conducted by the Religious of Saint Joseph Calascantius. The attendance is limited, but Rome abounds in schools for rich and poor.

FEBRUARY 22nd.—Another general congregation of the Council this morning. New regulations given to the Most Reverend Fathers. To the Irish College; and then to call upon the Countess de S——. Visit to St. Mary Major's, and home by the Trinta di Monte, Piazza d'Espagna, and the Via di Condotti, remarkable for the number and magnificence of its jewellery establishments;

across the Corso, and by the Pantheon, to our snug quarters, No. 57, Santa Chiara, opposite the French Seminary.

Immense crowds attending the Carnival—still in full blaze; and yet the churches are not forgotten. The "Forty Hours" prayer is being kept at the "Minerva," and many kneel in adoration before the God of the Eucharist—the "Word made flesh and dwelling amongst us."

FEBRUARY 23rd.—A red-letter day. Seven a.m. saw us *en route* for the far-famed Subiaco, forty-four miles from Rome, the cradle of the great Benedictine Family. The morning was clear and cold—very cold for this lovely climate: ice had formed in the gutters.

We rested and dined at Tivoli. The dinner might have been much better—considering the charges.

The Locanda della Sibilla is not celebrated for its *menu*—nor for cleanliness. Hunger is good sauce, however; we could not complain of our appetite. We visited—my second visit to this romantic place—the grottos of Neptune and the Sibyl, and reviewed with intense pleasure the Cascatelli, 320 feet in height, and of surpassing beauty. The waters can be likened to nothing more than immense streams of molten silver rapidly rushing down.

The classical associations of Tivoli render it peculiarly interesting to the scholar. Horace sang its praises, and here he longed to spend the evening of his life:—

"*Tibur Argœo positum Colono,*"
"*Sit meæ sedes utinam senectæ.*"
"*Sit modus lasso maris et viarum*"
"*Militiæque.*"
Lib. II. VI. 5.

After dinner we started for our destination, following the course of the Arno, or Teverone, which flows through a beautiful valley, towering above which, rise in the distance lofty mountains, their summits capped with snow, and offering a glorious appearance in the golden reflection of the setting sun.

Immense vineyards line the way; the vines generally supported by mulberry trees. Often they are trained from tree to tree, and in autumn, laden with their yellow and purple clusters, shaded by the dark green leaves, must produce a charming effect.

Between Tivoli and Subiaco we pass numerous small villages perched so high upon the mountains that one wonders how they can be reached.

In one of these, Vicovaro, in 1863, the eyes of a picture of the Madonna were seen to move; a fact witnessed by crowds of people. Saracinesco, whose inhabitants descend from the Saracens, defeated by Berengarius in the ninth century, is another of these charmingly picturesque towns, and towers over the river 2,500 feet. It was after seven when we reached Subiaco, where we put up at the Locanda della Pernice, whose accommodations made ample amends for the inn at Tivoli.

An excellent supper, a blazing fire on the hearth, for the evening was cold and our drive had chilled us, kept us in admirable mood, pleased with ourselves—and the world at large. Good, clean beds awaited us, from which we rose, bright and early next morning, after the long journey—forty-four miles—in a carriage.

The cathedral is dedicated to the Apostle St. Andrew; it was built by Pius VI., who had been abbot of the monastery for many years.

Like most of the churches in Italy, it is a fine building—but might be kept more carefully.

Having celebrated Mass, we made our thanksgiving, and witnessed the marriage of an Italian peasant couple.

The parties seemed very young and very poor. Still the bride looked interesting in her picturesque head dress and costume of many colors; and no doubt the future appeared to her as bright as to more favored ones, on such occasions.

After a slight breakfast at the hotel—the morning meal in Italy is generally very simple, a cup of coffee or chocolate, with bread and butter—we set out for the great Benedictine Monastery, the Sacro Speco. The ascent is steep, the scenery very grand; about one-half of the road is very good, accessible to carriages, the rest is done on foot without much fatigue.

This famous monastery of St. Benedict is about two and a quarter miles from the town, always ascending.

The view in every direction is magnificent, varied, almost wild.

Here, St. Benedict, a noble patrician youth, retired, A.D. 450, at the age of fourteen.

The monastery was rebuilt in 847; the lower church

dates from 1053, the upper from 1066, and the cloister from 1235.

It is built against the mountain's side, and contains many very beautiful chapels.

Beneath one of the altars are preserved a head and other relics of the Holy Innocents.

In the grotto in which St. Benedict passed three years is an exquisite statue of the saint in white marble, the work of Bernini.

On the ledge of the rock rests a sculptured basket of bread, recalling the legend of his food being let down to him when dwelling in this cave, by the monk Romanus.

A huge mass of rock overhangs the monastery; one would think it might fall at any moment, and really it seems miraculously upheld.

In the garden, a statue of the saint, his finger pointing to this enormous block, has this inscription upon its base: "Noli tangere filios meos"—touch not my children. Did it fall it must necessarily crush in the monastery. The monks, smiling, say: "There is no danger." Carefully enclosed by an iron railing there is a bed of roses—originally, it is said, thorns, in which, tradition says, St. Benedict rolled himself in order to extinguish the violence of his passions.

Be this as it may, certain it is, in each leaf is cut naturally, the form of a serpent. We have still some of these leaves. Our rev. guide, Padre Bruno, was a Prussian, and spoke English remarkably well. He received us most graciously. The principal church, dating from the fifteenth century, is richly frescoed. It has never been consecrated. Gregory IX., who consecrated the altar, saying, it was sacred enough in its founder, and St. Francis, of Assisium, who visited it in 1223.

Bidding adieu to the good monk, who embraced us as we left, we descended the mountain side and knocked at the gate of the ancient monastery of Santa Scholastica, founded in the fifth century, and restored by the Abbot Stephanus in 981.

In the cloister we saw a sarcophagus, found in Nero's villa, very elaborately wrought.

Under a portico is a fine bas-relief of a stag drinking from a sort of chalice, and having an inscription recording the erection of this monastery and church.

The recumbent statue of a saint in a crypt, lighted in some mysterious way, impressed us very much. This monastery was the first place in Italy where the printing press was established, by the Germans—Sengenheim and Pannartz.

The monks I met in these two monasteries were remarkably handsome, distinguished-looking men. The father who accompanied us through Santa Scholastica, seemed as if his features were chisselled; his complexion was beautiful, his eyes black and lustrous, with an expression that might well be said, "of the earth—unearthly." One might have fancied it was the angel guardian of this holy place, robed in the coarse but graceful habit of the children of St. Benedict.

The Abbot of this monastery is mitred; his throne in the church is just like a bishop's. His rank, a lord's.

These saintly men never eat meat, and within the cloister

observe perpetual silence. They may speak in the garden during recreation. Returning to Rome, we spent the night at Tivoli; said mass next morning in the Capuchin Church, and there visited the famous Villa d' Est, built by a cardinal of the name, son of Alfonso II., Duke of Ferrara.

We reached the eternal city towards evening, delighted with our excursion, replete with most agreeable souvenirs. The gentlemen whom I had the honor to accompany on this charming little tour, were, Monsieur de Fontenay, Grand Vicaire de Sens; Rev. Pére Daume —since dead—and Monsieur l'Abbé d'Aubichon, Student of the Sèminaire Français. More agreeable companions it would have been difficult to find, and their attention to me—the only stranger—was of the most marked, most delicate nature. What a pleasure—and a pleasure to look back to—to meet, associate with, and be familiar with real gentlemen!

FEBRUARY 27th.—With Mgr. Lootens, Vicar-Apostolic of Idaho, I visited to-day, St. Mary Major's, St. Sylvester's, San Martino di Monti, Santa Maria della Pace, and the Gesu—the great church of the children of St. Ignatius. In the latter magnificent basilica, the Quarante Ore, or Forty Hours', Devotion, was going on.

The grand altar was a blaze of light, thousands of great tapers being used in the illumination of the sanctuary, while the Blessed Sacrament was enthroned high above all, the centre of what seemed like a reflex of celestial glory. At the Mass, twenty-six cardinals, and many bishops were present. The singing was superb, and the great concourse of people seemed deeply absorbed in the grand religious ceremony, one of the most beautiful of the church.

San Martino stands upon the ruins of the Thermae of Trajan. It was built by St. Symmachus, A. D. 500, and on the site of a still more ancient church founded by St. Sylvester, in the time of Constantine.

The subterranean church—a part of those baths—was kindly shown to us by the clerics, who are always happy to oblige strangers, and invariably receive them with the greatest politeness. Hard by is the basilica Eudoxiana, on the Esquiline, as already mentioned, so called from the wife of Valentinian III., who built it in 442, during the pontificate of Gregory the Great, as a repository for the chains with which St. Peter had been bound at Jerusalem. "*Peter was sleeping between two soldiers, bound with two chains.*"—(Acts xii. 6.) Another pleasant evening at Madam M's.—a great rendezvous for Mgrs, and other distinguished persons—lay and clerical.

FEBRUARY 28th.—We spent the afternoon at the exhibition of Christian art—a grand display. The chief contributions were from France. The papal jewels, tiaras, etc., and the ancient mitres of Innocent III. and Urban VIII. excited considerable curiosity. We again witnessed the amusements of the carnival; the last day apparently being the best. A hundred thousand people must have been upon the streets, and as the beginning, so at the end of the carnival, everything passed off in the most orderly manner possible. The most beautiful statue at the exhibition was, to my taste, that of *Mater Admirabilis*—really admirable for its loveliness.

ASH WEDNESDAY.

MARCH 2nd.—Quite a change has come over the city. What a contrast after the noise, bustle and excitement of the carnival—the great holiday of the Romans. Lent is upon us, and evidently the mass of the people realize it is the holy season consecrated to penance and to prayer.

At St. Peter's the Pope blessed the ashes, and distributed them to the cardinals, a few of the bishops, and to some royal personages, who first kissed the Pontiff's feet. Several thousands were in the great basilica, but how few some thousands seem within those vast precincts!

Much satisfaction expressed to-day over the letter of the Bishop of Strasburg, condemning Pére Grattry, and *hoc genus omne*—oppositionists, who have received a blow from which they will not soon recover.

In the afternoon we visited the church of St. Alexis on Monte Aventino; venerated the great relic of the saint, and saw the staircase under which he lodged for seventeen years as a poor mendicant unrecognized, though in the palace of his father. Everyone should read his life. "Wonderful is God in His Saints."

Another interesting visit was to the church and cloister of St. Gregory the Great, on Monte Cœlio, and to that of St. John and St. Paul, where those great saints suffered martyrdom. In this latter church reposes the body of St. Paul of the Cross, founder of the Passionists, which is still well preserved, and lies under the altar for the veneration of all.

A superb chapel, a gem of the most beautiful mosaics and marbles, is being prepared for the reception of his sacred relics, which we had the happiness of venerating.

A delightful drive to the "Marmorata," on the bank of the Tiber, wound up this pleasant afternoon.

Their Lordships met this evening at the rooms of His Grace the Archbishop of Quebec, to transact business in connection with the church in Canada.

NAPLES.

MARCH 7th.—This morning the Abbé St. Aubin and I left Rome for Naples. We slept at Ancona, a seaport on the Adriatic, and early next morning went on by rail to Loreto, where we had the happiness to celebrate Mass in the *Santa Casa*, or Holy House of Nazareth. Padre Rosignoli received us most kindly; and after Mass allowed us to inspect the magnificent treasury of the basilica. The first Napoleon robbed this church of the value of 3,000,000 francs worth in gold, silver, precious stones and sacred ornaments.

From a balcony of the monastery the Padre pointed out to us the battle-field of Castel Fidardo, where many brave fellows lost their lives defending the rights of the Holy See.

Loreto is beautifully situated upon a lofty eminence, overlooking a lovely country. As we ascended the hill to the place of our pilgrimage we sang the "Ave Maris Stella," and, returning, the "Magnificat," "for the great things the Lord had done for us."

We reached Naples in the afternoon of the following day, taking up our quarters at the Hotel Central, where we had excellent accommodation, and reasonably too. Having dined, we strolled about the city, visited the quay, and had much pleasure on seeing in the harbor an English and American vessel both flying their familiar colors.

We invested in some oranges, just for the novelty,— "three for a penny,"—and while engaged in this mercantile transaction, one of the young gentlemen who are so numerous on the Neapolitan docks kindly relieved me of my immaculate pocket handkerchief. It was not a very serious loss, and about the only one from the time I left till I returned to Canada.

Next morning we "did" the royal palace, which, of course, is magnificent in all its appointments. The scala regia—royal staircase—is of marvellous beauty, and no doubt of marvellous cost.

As we sauntered through the apartments the guide

called our attention to a cradle—twelve thousand dollars worth—an immense tortoise shell, immensely ornate, the gift of the city to the Princess Margarita, now Queen of Italy, for the young prince, heir of the two Sicilies. From the terrace of the palace we had an unrivalled view of the lovely bay, the docks, much of the city, and Vesuvius in the distance.

The churches of this vast metropolis number nearly three hundred. We said Mass at Santa Chiara, the great St. Clare.

From the royal residence we drove to the splendid church and monastery of San Martino, which justly ranks among the most beautiful of Italian ecclesiastical structures, and perhaps the loveliest of the Neapolitan churches.

The paternal government of Victor Emmanuel had driven out the venerable Carthusians, leaving the sacred place in care of soldiers, quartered in the convent.

A very few, four or five, of the monks were allowed to remain still within its walls, but the community was disbanded. This really magnificent religious house commands probably the very best view of Naples and its environs, being situated upon a lofty hill overlooking the city and bay.

Deeply deploring the sad fate of the good fathers, we continued our drive to the great ruins of the palace of Sejanus, and passed through a vast and lofty tunnel by torch light. These ruins and the amphitheatre will repay a visit, and should be neglected by no tourist.

Where Virgil is said to have written, was pointed out; called *Scuola di Virgile*

Passing through the grotto of Pausilippe, we come to the poet's tomb; a plain stone, erected by a librarian of some queen of France, marks out what is said to have been the last resting-place of the author of the immortal Æneid.

MARCH 11th.—Off to Pompeii, fifteen miles from Naples, passing through many quaint villages that border the way.

As every one knows, this once great city was destroyed A. D. 79—by the eruption of Vesuvius, that poured its torrents of molten lava upon the unfortunate place. After spending considerable time examining the most interesting parts, so far unearthed, and witnessing the excavations still in progress, we took some little refreshments, and having procured horses and guides, ascended to the very top of the burning mountain, which is covered many feet deep with the finest, blackest ashes, and here and there huge pieces of lava ejected from the crater and still hot. Not a blade of grass is to be seen here, while lower down, near the base of the mountain, are fine vineyards that furnish a most delicious wine. The ascent, after leaving the horses, is exceedingly tiresome and difficult, but the fatigue is amply recompensed by the wondrous view of the country, land and sea.

My companion gave up before we reached the mouth of the crater; with the help of the guides I ascended to the very top. It has been said, " See Naples—and die."— Better, we think, as some one else has added, " See

Naples—and live to see it again." Certainly one could scarcely weary of this lovely city and its enchanting environs—whether on land or water. We returned to Rome by another route, and thus had a very good idea of some of the most beautiful parts of the fair land of Italy.

MARCH 15th.—Rome again; a most warm greeting from His Lordship, who was not a little lonely during my few days' absence.

Said mass this morning for my dear deceased brother, in the very room where St. Ignatius of Loyola, the founder of the illustrious Society of Jesus, breathed his last.

Some of his letters, as well as some written by St. Francis Borgia, St. Vincent de Paul, St. Philip Neri, and other saints, were kindly shown to us by the rev. custodian. In a large glasscase stands a life-size wax figure of St. Ignatius, said to be a perfect likeness, and robed in the very same vestments he so often used when offering the Holy Sacrifice of the Mass.

In the afternoon I visited Santa Maria in Trastevere, built by Pope Calixtus, A. D. 224; it was the first church dedicated in Rome to the Mother of God—"Our Mother also."

This is the basilica Cardinal Gibbons has received as his titular, and hence will have more than a passing interest for American Catholics. The following day my Mass was said at the grand altar of the Minerva, under which reposes the body of St. Catherine, of Sienna, one of the glories of the great Dominican order. After dinner I paid a visit to the chapel in the Masimo palace, where the raising to life of a young prince by Saint Philip Neri is every year most religiously commemorated. The place was thronged all day. On coming out we met the Pope taking his usual drive, and got his blessing. I consider myself singularly fortunate in meeting His Holiness so often. The shadow of the first Pope, St. Peter, restored health to the sick (Acts). The wave of the hand—making the sign of the cross over us—and the prayer and benediction from the heart and lips of his successor, must surely be powerful before God.

MARCH 17th.—St. Patrick's day, Ireland's great religious anniversary. My Mass this morning, as it has always been on this hallowed day, was offered for Ireland and Irishmen—the world over—God bless them! Should "Home Rule" come during my life, I shall flatter myself that the holy sacrifice offered regularly for so many years on the national festival has contributed not a little to obtain this great blessing for long suffering Ireland. I was delighted—it was in a small church, St. Ann's— to learn that at the same altar Pius IX. said his first Mass, April 8th, 1819, just fifty-one years before. The day was well observed, at St. Isidore's, *capo le case* the church of the Irish Franciscans. High Mass was sung by Bishop Shiels, of Australia, and the sermon, a very fine one indeed, by His Grace, the Archbishop of Westminster, now Cardinal Manning. This was really an eventful week, my next mass being celebrated in the room of St. Philip Neri. The very obliging Sacristan showed me the confessional, crucifix, and other things now precious as having belonged to this great servant of God, the Apostle of Rome.

MARCH 19th.—St. Joseph's day. At the altar dedicated to this great saint, I had the happiness of saying mass in the French seminary. At the grand altar, high mass was going on, a big negro priest, a native of Senegambia, Africa, being the celebrant, assisted by two ecclesiastics, as deacon and sub-deacon. His bishop, the saintly Kobez, an Alsatian by birth, was present and evidently delighted with his dear young priest, who, by the way, was blacker than any ace of spades. Holy Catholic Church, how worthy art thou of the world's admiration! Raising to thy altars the children of a despised, degraded race, and placing them among thy princes—the princes of thy people—that they may bring thy light and truth to their fellow creatures, sitting in darkness and in the shadow of death! Within thy bosom there is no distinction of persons; and never did that strike us more than when, during the sacred ceremony, we saw the lips of the handsome young priest who served as deacon, respectfully pressed to the hand of the African, as from him he received the glowing censer, and offered to him the blessed incense.

After mass, the rev. negro dined with the gentlemen of the seminary, and appeared to be the hero of the day. It was said he was very clever; he had just finished his studies at the Propaganda, and was soon to return, to bring the glad tidings of the gospel to his far off distant home.

MARCH 23rd.—An auspicious day, being received in audience by the Sovereign Pontiff. This was my second audience. The first was in December, and regarding it I find these remarks in my note-book.
" *Extract from a letter dated Rome, Dec. 20th,* 1869."

My letter written last week was too late for the mail; however, it's just as well, as it affords me an opportunity to let you know that last evening, His Holiness granted an audience to the bishops and priests of the Dominion, now in Rome.

Their Lordships were admitted first, and after a few minutes the Pope sent for the priests. I had the honor to kiss his foot, and when leaving, an opportunity to pass before His Holiness presented itself, of which you may be sure I availed myself; he gave me his hand, which I kissed most fervently.

His Holiness received us in the kindest manner, laying aside all ceremony. He stood the whole time by a table, having but two of the gentlemen of his household with him.

During the audience he talked and joked continually;

so much so that, were it possible, we might have forgotten, so great was his condescension, that we were in the presence of the Vicar of Jesus Christ, compared to whom all the kings of the earth are as nothing.

He blessed us with all the fervor of his soul in the following words, which made an impression on all who heard him. that will last as long as life.

We were all upon our knees, every sound was hushed, we scarcely breathed, lest we should lose one word of that blessing which all regarded as coming from God Himself.

Raising his eyes and hand, looking more like one just from heaven, than a mortal, he said :—" May the blessing of God the Father, and of the Son, and of the Holy Ghost descend upon you ; may it descend upon your clergy, your people, your religious communities, and upon your friends ; may this blessing remain with you all the days of your life : in the name of the Father, and of the Son, and of the Holy Ghost. Amen."

You know I am not an enthusiast; and yet I would willingly travel back to Rome to be blessed as I was blessed last night by the successor of St. Peter, and to feel once more the ineffable joy I experienced in this, to me, one of the most consoling occasions of my life."

Going to the audience to day—March the 23rd,—we passed the Gens d'Armes, and the Swiss Guards, in their quaint costumes, designed by Michael Angelo; we as-

cended the stair-case, crowned at its summit by the gorgeous stained glass windows, with full length figures of St. Peter and St. Paul, executed in the very highest perfection of such work, and presented to Pio Nono, by Maximilian II., King of Bavaria, and having the inscription:—
"*Pontifici Maximo, feliciter regnanti;*"—" To the Sovereign Pontiff, gloriously reigning."

We remained some time in an antechamber, a hall of vast dimensions, occupied by guards and other officials. We entered another apartment, and were finally admitted to the audience chamber.

Having a good hour to wait, we had ample time to take in the surroundings, and had some fine views from the windows of the Vatican Palace.

Suddenly one of the court officials entered, announcing the coming of the Pope. In a few moments His Holiness appeared, preceded by a chamberlain, and accompanied by two monsignors.

As usual, he wore the white cassock, over which was thrown a heavy cloak of scarlet cloth, edged with gold; a white silk cincture, the ends embroidered with a chalice in raised bullion, and red silk shoes, with the golden cross upon them. At the approach of the Holy Father, all knelt.

I was the first ecclesiastic to whom he spoke. He gave me his hand to kiss, after which I bowed and kissed his foot. Asking in Italian who I was, I answered in French: from Canada, Holy Father, diocese of Kingston.

He repeated the name a couple of times—Kingston—

Kingston—with a very foreign accent, without seeming to remember the place.

Noticing my Roman collar—the other ecclesiastics were French, and wore the 'rabbat,' peculiar to them—His Holiness tapped me on the breast, and evidently much pleased, said: O le Canada, le Canada—no doubt, thinking of her devotion to the Vicar of Christ and to Holy Mother Church.

The reverend gentlemen whom I accompanied to the audience were: l'Abbé Simonis, Curé de Riheim, l'Abbé Sester, Curé de Milhausen, and l' Abbé Meyer, all from Alsace, diocese of Strasbourg.

His Holiness was exceedingly gracious; speaking a word to each one, and looking very well, and very happy. He blessed us all, and, as he was leaving the throne-room, turned and said: " I have blessed and indulgenced the crucifixes and other pious objects."

MARCH 25th.—The great festival of the Annunciation of the Blessed Virgin Mary.

To-day the Sovereign Pontiff went, in *Grand Gala*, to the church of Santa Maria, Sopra Minerva, to attend the high mass, and afterwards distribute dowries to the young girls, portioned by the confraternity of the Annunziata.

The morning was lovely, and the papal cortege presented the grandest outdoor spectacle I ever beheld,

All Rome seemed to crowd the streets, through which

the gorgeous pageant passed, and the greatest enthusiasm everywhere was manifested.

The route from the Vatican to the church was covered with the bright yellow sand from Montorio, while flowers were strewn in the way, and fairly rained on the Pontiff's carriage. The Pope passed directly under our windows, affording us a long and complete view of this unrivalled ceremony.

The church was densely crowded, as indeed were also all the approaches to it.

The equipages of the cardinals, crimson and gold; the carriages of the foreign ambassadors, the noble and Swiss guards, the dragoons—the *tout ensemble* making a parade unequalled for splendor by anything of the kind in Europe.

After dinner I visited Sts. Cosma and Damian, enriched with mosaics, dating from A. D. 530, and Sta. Francesca Romana, built upon the site of the temples of Venus and Roma.

The tomb of the saint, by Bernini, is very elaborate, and is surmounted by her statue, guarded by two angels, a most costly and elegant work.

There is here a beautiful bas-relief, from designs by Pietro Oliviero, erected as a monument to Gregory XI. in 1584, by the Senate and people, in memory of the return of the papal court from Avignon, in 1377, after an absence of seventy-two years.

In the wall, protected by an iron grating, are two stones, deeply impressed, it is said, by St. Peter kneeling upon them, when Simon Magus was carried off by the demon.

The bell tower, or campanile, is a fine specimen of this class of mediæval edifices, being one of the best preserved of the period—13th century.

Another visit to the Coliseum, and with more pleasure than ever. Like St. Peter's, each time one enters this huge structure it grows upon us, seeming grander, vaster, and more and more immense.

I mounted several stories, walking slowly through and admiring this grandest of Roman ruins at leisure.

It covers six acres, the form is elliptical, the outer wall is 157 feet high; it accommodated a hundred thousand spectators. Here often flowed the blood of the early christians!

From its lofty walls may be had, in all directions, fine views of the city and all about it—a glorious panorama.

Returning, we visited the "Golden House" of Nero, with its ancient frescoes excellently preserved, after more than eighteen hundred years. The portions excavated are very large and very lofty, well repaying a visit. Nero left it incomplete, and Otho spent 30,000,000 sesterces merely to finish it. It is still magnificent in its ruins.

MARCH 28th.—To-day, His Holiness received Mgr. Kobez, Vicar Apostolic of Senegambia, in private audience. The saintly bishop brought with him his little negro valet, a very black, but very bright boy. The

Holy Father asked the young darkey to make the sign of the cross, and then saying, "*Introibo ad altare Dei*," to which the boy answered; the Pope, quite delighted, said, Un bon serviteur de messe pour le pape—a good one to serve the Pope's mass.

He pressed the little negro to his bosom, asked if he could say the Chaplet, and being answered in the affirmative, said, " well, I must give you one," and retiring for a moment, brought the lad a lovely rosary blessed by himself.

No wonder Pius IX. was venerated. Conscious of his dignity as Vicar of Christ; knowing it raised him far above all earthly princes, when he received them, he as a matter of course, often allowed them to prostrate themselves before him and kiss his feet; but here, he takes the little African, the boy servant of the humble bishop, and blesses, while he presses him to his heart. As our divine Lord said of Himself, so the Servus Servorum Dei —the servant of the servants of God—says: "Non quæro gloriam meam, sed ejus qui misit me." I seek not my own glory, but His who sent me. But with the poor and lowly he imitates the humility of his Master. Calling to-day upon a friend, near the Farnese palace, I had the pleasure of meeting Madame la Comtesse de G——, and her neice Mademoisille du M——. .

People from America cannot help being most favorably impressed by the grace and affability that distinguish so many of the nobility that one meets in Rome. The affectation and silly airs so often assumed by parvenus, are quite foreign to the genuine stamp. This struck me more and more forcibly each time I came in contact with those really noble people. Visited Mgr. Grimly at the Palazzo Caldorari, who was always delighted to see me.

MARCH 31st.—Bishop Horan, Bishop Larocque and I, to-day accompanied the Archbishop of Quebec, Mgr. Baillargeon, to Civita Vecchia, whence he was to sail for Canada.

His Grace was looking very ill; evidently a cause of great anxiety to his good Vicar-General, the present Cardinal, who was most sincerely and devotedly attached to Monseigneur. Who could help loving such a man! I thought I should never again see him—a fear that was realized. His Grace died in the autumn, October 13th, 1870—a real loss for the Church of Canada. On this trip I had the pleasure of making the acquaintance of the commander of the United States man-of-war—the *Franklin*, who kindly invited me to visit his vessel, then at Spezzia.

He had been thirty-seven years in the navy, and still looked fresh and young. He was a remarkably handsome man, of most agreeable manners and elegant conversation. We dined at Civita-Vecchia, and returned to Rome about half-past five, after a most pleasant day.

Mgr. Larocque, then Bishop of St. Hyacinth, Canada, was admittedly one of the handsomest men at the Vatican Council; Bishop Farrell of Hamilton was also much admired. They have both since "gone into the house of their eternity." May they rest in peace.

APRIL 1st.—A dark, gloomy day, anything but what one would expect in this usually beautiful climate. A most interesting visit this afternoon to the baths of Caracalla, situated between the Appian Way and the north-eastern declivity of the Aventine. They were begun by Caracalla about the year 240 ; enlarged and completed by Heliogabalus and Alexander Severus. These baths are the most perfect of any similar edifice in Rome, covering an area of 140,000 square yards. Olimpidorus states that they could accommodate sixteen hundred bathers at a time.

They form an immense square, surrounded by porticoes, and promenades planted with trees, and great halls devoted to gymnastics.

With the exception of the Coliseum, no ruins in Rome impress one more strongly with an idea of the ancient grandeur and magnificence of the capital of the world.

Many works of art have been found here. The Farnese Hercules, the huge Flora, the Torso Farnese, now in the Museum at Naples; the Atreus and Thyestes, the two gladiators, the Venus Callipsyge, now in the Vatican, and many other beautiful works, bronzes, cameos, bas-reliefs, medals, etc., etc. The poet Shelley loved to visit these wonderful ruins. In the preface to the " Prometheus Unbound," he says: " This poem was chiefly written upon the mountainous ruins of the baths of Caracalla, among the flowery glades and thickets of odoriferous blossoming trees which are extended in ever winding labyrinths, upon its immense platforms, and dizzy arches suspended in the air. The bright blue sky of Rome, and the effects of the vigorous awakening spring in that divinest climate, and the new life with which it drenches the spirits even to intoxication, were the inspiration of the drama."

From the baths we drove to the very ancient church of Saints Nereus and Achileus, mentioned in the year 494 under the title *Fasciola*—bandage.

A tradition says that St. Peter passing here, a piece of linen fell off his wounds, and a small mound arose, marking the spot.

Others think Fasciola a corruption of Fabiola, the Roman matron converted by St. Jerome, who gave her house in order that a church might be erected upon its site. Pope John I. rebuilt this church in 523; and Leo III. reconstructed it, a second time, in the ninth century. It was here Cardinal Baronius deposited the bodies of Saints Nereus and Achileus, with that of Saint Flavia Domitilla, which Gregory IX. had confided to the Church of St. Adrian.

The walls are beautifully frescoed, representing the history of the apostles. The altar and candelabra are very rich; and a magnificent Ambone, taken from the Church of St. Sylvester in Capite, is well preserved. Here also is the pontifical chair of St. Gregory the Great—in which I had the honor to sit—and from which he delivered his twenty-eighth homily; a portion of which is engraved on the back of the marble chair. The Vicar-General of Meaux (this was the great Bossuet's see), accompanied me in my rambles this afternoon. This distinguished ecclesiastic was quite at home amid the ruins; a most interesting guide and charming companion. Together we studied the antiquities.

APRIL 2nd. — Saturday — eve of Passion Sunday.— This morning in company with Mgr. Horan, I went to say Mass at the tomb of the Apostles. The Chapel of the Confession, as it is called, is immediately beneath the high altar of St. Peter's, and consequently directly under the wondrous dome; a fitting monument, overshadowing the sacred spot where rest the sacred relics of the prince of the apostles, and of his companion, the apostle of the gentiles.

In the fourth century, St. Cornelius brought hither the remains of St. Peter from the subterranean crypt of St. Sebastian, on the Appian Way.

Clement VIII. enriched the hallowed shrine with precious stones and costly ornamentation. Over the altar are two paintings of St. Peter and St. Paul, dating from the pontificate of Calixtus II. (1122). We reached St. Peter's about 8 o'clock, and it was nearly 12 before I began my Mass, so many dignitaries had to pass before me.

While awaiting my turn I heard eight Masses, recited the 'Little Hours' with other prayers, and the chaplet fifteen times, for the intentions for which I was about to offer the holy sacrifice.

It is seldom one's *preparatio ad missam* is so long, yet I found it not at all tedious, so delighted was I to realise one of the holiest desires of a priest's life—Mass at the tomb of the apostles.

One of the bishops who said Mass that morning belonged to some oriental rite.

He wore a cope instead of a chasuble, and after the consecration, holding the Sacred Host in his left hand, which rested on the chalice, he turned towards the assistants, and raising his voice, struck his breast thrice with the greatest solemnity. The ceremony of course was new to me; but was as impressive as it was novel.

The eastern bishops for the most part are venerable looking men; their vestments tend not a little, by their amplitude and magnificence, to enchance the nobility of their appearence.

The Greeks wear a crown, as the Latins wear a mitre; it has certainly the advantage over the latter, which becomes so very few men.

We ended this day, so well begun, at the "Orti-Farnesiani," among the ruins of the palace of Vespasian, the temples of Jupiter Victor, and Jupiter Stator, the palace of Tiberius, the palace of Caligula, the site of the house of Romulus. In fact, we had in view the kingly, republican and imperial periods, each manifested in its crumbling ruins, striking memorials of the vanity of all earthly grandeur.

APRIL 3.—Passion-Sunday. We have reached the last fortnight of Lent. Great anticipations for Holy Week, the ceremonies of these days being one of the chief attractions for strangers in Rome.

All on the *qui vive*, hoping the offices will be at St. Peter's, instead of the Sixtine chapel, which admits of very few comparatively.

An interesting visit to-day to the national church of the Germans, Santa Maria dell 'Anima, which is under the special protection of Austria. Also, to Santa Maria della Pace, built by Sixtus IV. in 1482, in commemoration of the peace of Christendom, threatened by the Turks in 1480.

Here are seen the four Sibyls of Raphael;—the Cumaean, Persian, Phrygian and Tiburtine; acknowledged by all connoissuers as some of the most perfect work of the immortal master. The noble family of the Chigi have here a very beautiful chapel, designed by Michael Angelo.

About 4 o'clock the Pope drove to the Sessorian Basilica, Santa Croce in Gerusalemme, for the consecration of the *Agnus Dei*. A great crowd had assembled, and cheered the pontiff lustily, as he descended from his carriage and again, as he was leaving, at the conclusion of the ceremony.

But after all, how unreal are these ovations! How soon the hozannas of Palm Sunday are succeeded by the crucifige, of Good Friday! and how often, oh, how often! has not the paternal heart of Pio Nono had reason to bleed for the ingratitude of a wayward, fickle, easily intimidated people.

April 6th.—Yesterday, at the Quirinal, I had the honor of being presented to His Eminence Cardinal Berardi, Minister of Public Works for the pontifical government.

The amiable simplicity, the affability, the gracious dignity of those real princes of the Church, charms every-one, and shows how naturally true worth excludes all attempt or aiming to make others feel its superiority.

The cardinals' apartments in the apostolic palace were handsomely, but not luxuriously, furnished.

To-day, the Lenten Station was held at the gorgeous Church of San Marcello, on the Corso—Rome's finest street, and at one time universally allowed to be the finest street in Europe.

Leaving here, we went on to Santa Maria, in Via-lata, and visited the prison in which St. Paul was kept; we brought away a little of the water from the well, there existing in his time.

April 7th.—Said mass this morning at St. Ignatius' Church, part of the Roman College, and at the very tomb of the dear little Saint Louis de Gonzaga, remembering it was on his feast, 21st of June, 1858, that for the *first time* I offered the adorable sacrifice in the chapel of the Hotel Dieu, Kingston.

I called this afternoon at the palace of His Eminence Cardinal Patrizi, Vicar-General of His Holiness, and acting Bishop of Rome, who graciously authorized me to get some of the sacred relics from the custode. His Lordship, Bishop Horan, brought them out on his return from Rome.

All this week, near San Augustino's, in a lovely chapel, hung with crimson and gold and other tasteful decorations, a vast number of precious relics from the catacombs are exposed for the veneration of the faithful who, judging from the constant throng, deeply appreciate the privilege.

Went to the "Dogana,"—Custom House—on business for Monseigneur.

APRIL 8th.—During Lent there is each day, at some of the great churches, what is marked in the Roman Missal—*Statio apud Sanctum Petrum*, etc., etc.

To-day this Statio was held at San Stefano, in Rotondo, so called from its circular form.

This church crowns the Coelian hill, to the west, and is one of the most remarkable in Rome.

It is not supposed to have been built originally for ecclesiastical purposes; 'tis probably an ancient edifice.

The best opinion is, that it was the circular portion of the Macellum Grande, or great meat market, built in the time of Nero.

Pope St. Simplicius is said to have consecrated it to religion, in the year 464. The interior, which is 133 feet in diameter, has fifty-six columns: twenty in the inner, and thirty-six in the outer circle. The walls are covered with immense frescoes, depicting the martyrdoms of the different saints, from St. Stephen, the first martyr, to the reign of Julian, the apostate. The paintings are anything but artistic, yet very striking, and attract many visitors.

There is another basilica of St. Stephen, founded in the pontificate of St. Leo, in the middle of the fifth century, which was discovered during some excavations made in 1858.

Drove out with the Bishop and afterwards took a walk up to the capitol, visiting the Church of Santa Maria Liberatrice, templum di Vesta and the templum di Fortuna Virili. Thence to the Ponte-Rotto, and home by the Forum Romanum, descending the Capitoline Hill.

APRIL 10th.—Palm Sunday. My mass, yesterday, was said in the room, now a little oratory, where died the youthful saint Stanislaus de Kostka, at San Andrea della Quirinale, the Jesuits' novitiate in Rome. This morning I accompanied his Lordship to St. Peter's, for the ceremony of the blessing of the palms.

The Bishop received one from the Pope, which he most kindly presented to me.

The palms are prepared by the nuns and beautifully platted. Mine was over four feet long; very handsome, and is still, after eighteen years, most religiously preserved.

Probably thirty thousand people assisted at the ceremony. His Holiness looked magnificently; one would think he was really triumphing in the triumph of his Lord, commemorated upon that great day.

The Pope's choir sang the "Passion," to which it was impossible to listen with dry eyes.

At the elevation of the Host, the troops grounded arms; every sound was hushed within the vast basilica, and during the adoration a pin falling might be heard by the assembled thousands.

The profound silence is something wonderful, succeeding the sort of murmur, like waves gently breaking upon the shore, that is so remarkable at St. Peter's, when those great crowds are gathered beneath its glorious dome.

The "golden rose," destined for some royal lady, if one be found worthy of it, was borne before His Holiness, in a splendid vase, and placed at the foot of the cross, upon the altar, at which the Cardinal Archbishop of Bordeaux, Monseigneur Donnet, officiated.

I had the honour of an introduction to His Eminence, at the Quirinal Palace, where he resided during the Council. His manner was most charming. He seemed delighted to see people from Canada, the more than worthy daughter of his own fair France.

APRIL 11th.—Another red-letter day. Thanks to the politeness of Monsieur l'abbé Glaston, de Nimes, who had obtained the much sought favour from the Cardinal Vicar, and who had kindly invited me, I had the rare privilege of celebrating mass this morning in the catacombs of

Saint Calixtus, on the Appian Way, the vastest and probably the most important of all those that surround the eternal city.

Few enlightened travellers fail to visit this sacred spot, hallowed by the precious relics of 174,000 martyrs, who, after shedding their blood for Jesus Christ, found here a last resting-place.

The entrance to the catacombs is from a vineyard belonging to the pontifical government.

A broad stair-case, constructed probably when Constantine gave freedom to the Church, leads into the catacombs.

There the Christians of the fourth and fifth centuries came in crowds to visit the subterranean chapels and venerate the relics of the saints and martyrs.

There are four storeys—we might call them—some having as many as nine tiers of graves, or rather receptacles for the bodies.

The vestibule is covered with Greek and Latin inscriptions, all more or less proving that in those early days, as in the days of the Maccabees, and at the present day in the Catholic Church, it was believed to be a "holy and a wholesome thought to pray for the dead, that they may be loosed from their sins."

The crypt of the popes, discovered in 1851, by Signor Rossi, is particularly interesting.

Fragments of sepulchral monuments are here inscribed with the names of several pontiffs, in Greek characters, whose bodies were deposited in this place.

Eutychianus, A. D. 275; Anterus, A. D. 235 : Fabianus A.D. 236; and Lucius, A.D. 232.

At the end stands the altar of the crypt, on which was offered the holy sacrifice of the Mass.

There is an inscription composed by St. Damasus, alluding to the popes buried here, ending with a wish to be laid near them himself, but which, in his respect and humility, he dared not aspire to :—

"Hic fateor Damasus volui mea condere membra,
Sed cineres timeo sanctos vexare Piorum."

To the left a narrow passage leads to the Chapel of St. Cecilia.

It was here we celebrated Mass; the altar being placed within a few feet of the Arcosolium, in which is a Sarcophagus, cut in the rock tufa that contained the body of the saint, therein deposited by Pope Urban, after her martyrdom.

Paschal I. removed her relics to the church built on the site of her palace, in the Trastevere, where they now repose before the grand altar, under the beautiful statue by Stefano Maderno.

This interesting sanctuary also owes its discovery to to the indefatigable archaeologist, de Rossi.

The pictures of several saints adorn the place. Three, Policamus, Sebastianus and Cyrinus, are designated by their names.

There is also a painting of a beautiful young woman, robed in richest apparel, laden with bracelets and necklaces, a type of the wealthy Roman ladies, and which is supposed by all to represent St. Cecilia.

Saint Urban, in pontifical vestments, his name clearly cut, is also to be seen depicted upon the wall.

A fresco represents the head of Our Lord, in the Byzantine style, and surmounted by a glory. These paintings date from the sixth or seventh century.

Among the many chapels generally visited, is found a most remarkable fresco, not later than the third century.

A fish bears upon its back a basket filled with small breads, and a bottle containing red wine.

We know the fish represents the Saviour; the bread and wine typify the sacred species of the Eucharist.

No doubt, this reminded the initiated of the adorable mystery of God's love for man.

Thus the faithful of the second century, like the faithful of the nineteenth century, firmly believed in the real presence of Jesus Christ, under the appearances of bread and wine.

We often wonder, but then, faith is a gift of God, and *Spiritus spirat ubi vult*—the Spirit breatheth where he will—how people who believe the New Testament can possibly doubt this most consoling dogma of our holy religion.

They hesitate not to admit that the Holy Ghost, who is God, descended upon Jesus Christ, when baptised in the Jordan, under the *appearance of a dove*; and that a voice from heaven was heard saying, "This is my beloved Son, in whom I am well pleased."

They believe that the same divine person came upon the apostles on the day of Pentecost under the *form of tongues of fire*. Now, if God the Holy Ghost could assume *these appearances* and *be really present under them*, which must be admitted, or reject the New Testament entirely, for if it be untrue in part, what guarantee have they it is not wholly untrue,—who can doubt that God the Son could give Himself to us, and *be really present under the appearances of bread and wine?* Surely nothing is impossible to God; and the three Divine persons are but one God; and of the three, no one is more powerful than the other. Oh! let people ask for faith! it is truly the gratuitous gift of God, but never refused to those who lead pure lives, and ask it with humility and sincerity.

The chapel, sometimes called of the Sacraments, is well worthy of more than a passing visit.

. There are three beautiful and remarkable frescoes. The Good Shepherd—a figure often seen in the catacombs, is carrying a lamb upon his shoulders; on each side are sheep that an apostle is trying to bring to his master; one turns away disdainfully, the other is looking and listening attentively; a third is brousing; but the rain of heaven falls gently upon them all. Another fresco represents Moses striking the rock; in the third, Jesus Christ is seen, between two disciples, multiplying the loaves and fishes.

The Good Shepherd recalls the sacrament of penance; the water gushing from the rock, reminds us of the sacrament of baptism; and the multiplication of the loaves and fishes, speaks to the Christian soul, of the most adorable sacrament of the altar.

It will, no doubt, interest our readers to learn how the Chevalier de Rossi made these important discoveries.

After Pope Cornelius, who lived in the middle of the third century, had suffered martyrdom at Civita Vecchia, his body was transported to Rome by a noble lady of the city, and deposited in the cemetery of Saint Calixtus.

The same day, but not the same year, Saint Cyprian was shedding his blood for the faith in Africa, and the faithful to whom he had announced the word of God, gathered up and preserved his precious remains.

The Church of Rome re-unites these two saints, celebrating their festival on the same day, 16th of September.

In the mean time, all track was lost of the crypt that had received the relics of Saint Cornelius.

In 1851, a piece of a marble slab was found in the vineyard covering the cemetery of Saint Calixtus, on which was inscribed: ELIVS MARTYR.

De Rossi, to whom was brought the inscription, at once came to the conclusion that it belonged to the tomb of Saint Cornelius.

In fact, it was known for certain that the cemetery contained the bodies of the popes of the third century.

Search was immediately made; excavations begun, and soon they came upon a stair-case of twenty-four steps, one of those constructed in the fourth century, to facilitate access to the shrines of the martyrs.

As he advanced, numberless names and inscriptions presented themselves. Soon he perceived a crypt, near which, lying on the ground he noticed another fragment of marble, fitting perfectly with the one already found in the vineyard, having the letters: CORNEP ;—exactly what was wanted to complete the inscription: CORNELIVS MARTYR EP (iscopus).

So that at last they had the sepulchral tablet of Saint Cornelius.

Above, a coarse painting represented St. Cornelius in pontifical robes, and St. Cyprian, both holding in their hands the book of the gospels.

All doubt was now removed ; they found themselves in possession of the *loculus* where the body of the saint had been deposited.

To the right, before the *Cubiculum*, is seen a pillar, on which stood the lamp that burned at the martyr's tomb. This oil was considered precious, since it is mentioned in the list of gifts sent by Pope St. Gregory the Great to Theodolinda, and bequeathed by her to the Cathedral of Monza, where it was designated—*ex oleo Sancti Cornelii*.

Before returning home, we inspected the *Columbariums* on the Appian Way, and the tombs of the Scipios.

The morning was delightful ; and the scent of the lilacs and flowers innumerable, made the air heavy with their exquisite perfume.

We came home by the Jewish quarter, charmed with this morning's instructive excursion.

To-day a letter appeared from the pen of Bishop Spalding, which produced a very good effect upon some of the Right-Rev. Fathers, and gave much satisfaction to all, in favour of the proclamation of the dogma, which no one pretended to doubt, but which many considered inopportune—the infallibility of the Pope.

Purchased some very pretty mosaics at Noci's, 64 Via Fontanella di Borghese. Threatening rain; towards evening hot and very oppressive.

APRIL 12th.—Tuesday of the Great Week. My Mass to-day was celebrated at the Passionists' Monastery, near St. John's, of Lateran.

Within the convent, the Religious preserve the *Scala Santa*, the stairs taken from the palace of Pontius Pilate, and which the Redeemer of the world ascended and descended four times, on the morning of His passion; first, on arriving at the Roman governor's; then, going to and from Herod's; finally, after having been condemned to death, clothed with the mantle of derision and wearing the crown of thorns. It is composed of twenty-eight steps of white veined marble, unknown in Italy, but much used in Syria.

An ancient tradition, and which still exists in the Eastern Church, relates that the Empress Helena brought them from Jerusalem, with three doors and two pillars, to be placed in the Lateran palace.

The steps, to preserve them, are covered with heavy

plank; but an opening on the face of each allows one to see the marble and to touch it with the hand.

Pilgrims ascend the stairs upon their knees, descending by parallel stairs on each side.

Many and great indulgences are attached to this act of devotion. I ascended them twice—a very fatiguing thing —a goodly penance.

Having reached the top, we come to the *Sancta Sanctorum*, the ancient chapel of the popes, which had escaped when the palace was destroyed by fire.

Here are venerated the celebrated picture of our Saviour, life-size, painted on cedar and olive wood, styled the *Archiropoieta* (not made by the hand of man), and the *Sacra Tavola*, begun by St. Luke, and, according to the legend, finished by angels. It was transported in the fourth century from Jerusalem to Constantinople, where it remained in the greatest veneration up to the time of Leo the Isaurian.

Miraculously saved from the Iconoclasts, it reached Rome under the pontificate of Gregory I., who conveyed it to the patriarchate of Latran, the chapel of St. Lawrence.

At the foot of the Santa Scala, one on each side, stand two magnificent statues in white marble, the munificent gift of His Holiness Pius IX., one of which has the inscription, "*Haec est hora eorum et potestas tenebrarum,*" —" This is their hour and the power of darkness"; and the other—" *Osculo filiun hominis tradis?*"—" Dost thou betray the Son of Man with a kiss?" A just and scathing rebuke to the " Powers " that have, to their own perdition, like Judas, betrayed the Vicar of Jesus Christ.

To-day the first voting took place in the Aula of the Council. Terrible rain, accompanied by fearful thunder and lightning.

APRIL 13th.—Wednesday in Holy Week. At half-past four I assisted at the Tenebrae, in St. Peter's. The singing of the Lamentations by the papal choir was grand beyond conception ; the *Misercre*—something unearthly.

The same may be said of the office, next evening, though perhaps more thrilling. The *Miserere* had more of that wail, of which we have so often read; one might imagine it the last cry for mercy, the outpouring of the anguish of the souls of the dead. One's flesh fairly creeps, a chill comes over you, and the very blood seems to grow cold, as you listen to those accents of woe, echoing through the vast basilica and piercing the very marrow of one's bones. Nearly all the bishops attending the Council were present, and of course, added much to the grandeur and sublimity of this great function of the church.

The vast concourse of people seemed much affected ; and indeed, cold must be the heart and well nigh dead the faith of any who can assist unmoved at such a scene.

Holy Thursday, a Cardinal celebrated the High Mass, and the Pope, after carrying the most adorable Sacrament to the Chapel of the Canons, where it reposed till the ceremony of the next day, ascended to the Loggia and gave the papal benediction, *Urbi et Orbi*, and to the multitude kneeling on the great square of St. Peter's.

It was truly a grand sight. The day was lovely and the sky the clearest I had yet beheld. In the afternoon I visited many churches to see the "Repositories"; nothing very striking in any of them. I saw none to equal those of Quebec or Montreal.

APRIL 15th.—Good Friday.—Again to St. Peter's to assist at the great ceremonies of this day of days. An immense concourse of the faithful. I was particularly fortunate in securing a splendid position, near the column of St. Veronica, whence I could follow the grand function. One of the Cardinals officiated, and the sublime ritual of the Church was magnificently conducted. As on Palm Sunday, the Passion was rendered with admirable effect. The stillness of the vast multitude was almost oppressive. Earth has no more magnificent voices than those composing the Pope's choir, and following the words of the sacred writer, the chanting produced on me an impression beyond the power of language to describe. His Holiness came for the sermon, which was delivered by a 'Conventual,' occupying only fifteen minutes. The discourse was in Latin. Never have I seen in our pulpits anything approaching the gracefulness of gesture displayed on this occasion. I suppose it was really what the French call—*Un Sermon de circonstance.* After the adoration of the cross, the Sovereign Pontiff bore back the Sacred Host from the Canons' Chapel, and the service was resumed.

In several churches I saw to-day a carpet spread near the gate of the Sanctuary, with a cushion, and a crucifix, surrounded with lights and flowers, laid upon it. The people, on their knees, approached and kissed the marks of the sacred wounds.

Each evening, at the close of the "Tenebrae," the great relics of the Passion ;—the sacred lance, the towel impressed with the face of our Lord, and the wood of the True Cross were exposed, for the veneration of the faithful, from the balcony of St. Veronica.

In the afternoon of this thrice holy day, I had again the ineffable happiness of ascending, on my knees, the Scala Santa, and touching with my hands, the very steps, sanctified four different times—just 1837 years ago (1870), by the sacred feet, and stained by the precious blood of the Redeemer of the world.

O Rome, Alma Roma! had'st thou nothing else, would not such a privilege more than compensate the Christian for a journey from the uttermost ends of the earth!

From this venerable sanctuary, which was crowded by devout worshippers, I went on to the Coliseum, and made the "Holy Way of the Cross," in that place consecrated by the blood of countless martyrs, who within its walls gave their lives for God and Holy Church.

Nothing can be more touching than this great devotion, within this vast enclosure, majestic in its ruins, from whose galleries the emperors and the Roman people witnessed the heroism of the dying Christians; nothing more calculated to recall the most terrible souvenirs, while at the same time, nothing can give greater consolation to the Christian, Catholic heart.

Every Friday evening the devotions of the Stations of the Cross are performed in the Coliseum.

Thousands made the Stations here to-day. As I was leaving, a procession entered, headed by the Bishop Spaccapietra who, bareheaded, was carrying the cross. Soon after came another, the cross-bearer being the Princess Borghese, supported on each side by a noble lady. .

In the evening, at 8 o'clock, I accompanied several French priests to the Hospitium—*Trinita delli Peligrini*—and witnessed what can be seen no where but in Rome, in every sense the capital of the Christian world. Cardinals, princes, bishops, priests, noblemen, and other gentlemen, upon their knees, were washing the feet—and oh! such feet!—methinks I see them still, and still feel the overpowering atmosphere of the vast halls,—of hundreds of poor men and boys, pilgrims to the Holy City, come for the "Great Week," and afterward serving them at table, a most excellent supper being provided.

The halls of this institution are very fine, adorned with statues of the popes and inscribed with the names of the benefactors of this world-renowned refuge. The women were attended in their wards by princesses and other distinguished ladies, who are only too happy to perform this "labor of love." Many foreigners gazed upon this great charity, and appeared deeply impressed with the touching sight—that vividly recalled the ages of faith, when such heroic actions were the rule, not the exception.

HOLY SATURDAY.

This morning, I again ascended the Scala Santa (the indulgences are immense), and then at Saint John's of Lateran, witnessed the baptism of a Jew, a Jewess, and another convert. The ceremony was very imposing. It was here Constantine was baptized. Here I renewed my baptismal promises: may I be faithful to them! At this Mass, fifteen priests were ordained; His Eminence Cardinal Patrizi officiating, and getting through the many ceremonies in a wonderfully short time. Returning to the Monastery of the Passionists, I saw the procession of the Blessed Sacrament, and procured from one of the venerable fathers some of the oil from the lamps that ever burn before the miraculous image of our Saviour—in that place, than which—the inscription hath it:—" Non est sanctior locus in toto orbe terrarum "—" *There is no holier place in the whole world* "—and we well believe it. The popes resided for some time at the Lateran; here too several Councils were held—the fourth held in the year 1215—under Pope Innocent III.—defining the Easter-duty.

'Tis but a short drive from this to Santa-Croce, beyond the porta San Giovanni—St. John's gate. On the way are seen the ruins of the Roman acqueducts, time-worn and ivy-grown—yet still pretty well preserved—and, if I mistake not, some being still used for their original purposes.

EASTER SUNDAY.

APRIL 17th, 1870.—I was awakened this morning by the booming of the cannons of the castle of Saint Angelo, and the ringing of all the bells of the three hundred and sixty-five churches of the city, announcing the dawn of the glorious Easter day; truly the day which the Lord has made for His people, and on which we should be glad and rejoice. Having said my Mass, which, by the way, was served by a young Prussian, a splendid looking fellow, formerly a Zouave, and then studying for the African mission, Senegambia, and having attended Monseigneur at his, we drove to St. Peter's.

Already a vast multitude had assembled, and a few moments after we entered, the Sovereign Pontiff was borne in the Sede Gestatoria to his throne, while the most ravishing music was executed in the tribune above the great door.

His Holiness sang mass, and sang it so as to be heard throughout the immense basilica.

Fortunately I had an excellent place near the confession, and could see every movement of the Pope, and follow closely all the ceremonies of the Mass.

At the elevation of the Host, the troops, lining the church, presented arms. Every knee was bent, every sound hushed, every breath seemd stilled; and then, from the "wondrous dome" came the sounds of the silver trumpets, like the voices of celestial spirits, filling the soul with a flood of melody such as one may never again elsewhere expect to hear, and which we fancy can be rivalled only by the choirs of Heaven.

The "consecration" over, St. Peter's sent forth its multitudes, all anxious to secure a favorable position to witness the imposing rite of the Easter Benediction. I was among the fortunate ones on this memorable occasion. From the doors of the great temple to the extremity of the grand piazza, were congregated people from all parts of the world. It reminded one of the first Pentecost at Jerusalem. It was said that day, over two hundred thousand persons were within sight of the 'Vicar of Christ—truly the father of the faithful. Well might He say: "Thou hast given to me all the nations of the earth." Three splendid bands were present, and the troops under arms, drawn up upon the square.

A murmur runs through the vast crowd—every eye is raised to the tribune over the great portal of the world's greatest temple. At length, the cross—the sign of man's redemption—is seen above the "Loggia"; the papal attendants place the tiaras and mitres upon the marble balustrade, when, a few moments more, and the Pope appears, seated upon the portable throne, the great fans of ostrich feathers—the flabelli—waving on either side in the gentle breeze of this lovely morning.

The usual prayers are chanted; and then the Pontiff rises, raises his eyes and hands to heaven, and in tones, strong, sonorous, powerful and clear, gave the apostolic benediction, *Urbi et Orbi*—*to the city and to the world.*

Never, since the day of the transfiguration, did mortal eye gaze upon a more glorious sight! Well might we exclaim with the first of the Pontiffs—"Lord, it is well for us to be here."

No language can convey an idea of this magnificent spectacle. The noble piazza, with its silvery fountains, densely crowded; the splendour of the pontifical court; the gorgeous robes of the cardinals; the purple and gold of the bishops and minor prelates; the glitter of the uniforms of the military and the diplomatic corps; the great colonnade enclosing all within its mighty arms; the strains of delicious music; the religious enthusiasm of the assembled thousands;—and all this, in the "divinest of climates," beneath a cloudless sky—the "clear blue sky of Italy," went to make up a sight that can be seen only in Rome, and in Rome only at Easter or on Christmas Day.

THE ILLUMINATIONS.

"The illuminations of St. Peter's took place at 8 p.m. No one that has ever witnessed them can possibly forget the impressions produced by this magnificent display. Three hundred and eighty-two men are employed to light the lamps; the cost amounts to 3,000 lire.

"The first, called the *silver* illumination, begins at dusk, and consists of 5,900 lanterns; the second, called the *golden*, begins at 8 o'clock, on Easter night, when, on the signal being given, 900 lamps are lighted so instantaneously that it seems the work of enchantment.

"The whole is completed in about eight seconds; the entire building being then lit up by no less than 6,800 lamps. The lanterns used for the silver illumination are of white paper; those for the golden are iron cups filled with blazing tallow and turpentine.

"Every column, cornice and frieze; the bands of the dome, and all the details of the basilica to the summit of the cross, 448 feet high, are bright with lines of lamps and its gigantic architecture stands out against the dark sky in a firmament of fire."

No language can adequately describe this illumination, of which Rome and the Romans are so justly proud. Many have written about it, and the whole world has heard of it; but it must be seen to be realized.

Monday night, at the Piazza del Popolo, there was a grand display of fire-works; the French stating they had never seen their equal even in Paris, where this sort of thing is produced on the grandest scale.

Wednesday night the whole city was illuminated in honor of the Pope.

We cheered His Holiness as he drove by our carriage, inspecting the illuminations. He did not fail to bless us as he passed. The whole city seemed to be on foot, and yet everything was as orderly and decorous as the most exacting could desire. Rome, under the Popes, was truly a model city. During the five months I passed within its walls, I heard of only one very, very serious crime, and then there were certainly very extenuating circumstances.

Upon the streets no unbecoming sights meet the eye; no vile language offends the ear.

"ADIEU."

APRIL 23rd.—To-day, accompanied by Lieutenant Murray, I called upon the Canadian bishops to say "good bye." Noble Hugh Murray has since entered into his rest, leaving behind him a name honored by all who were privileged to know him. A brave soldier, a perfect gentleman, and a most devoted child of holy Mother Church. May his soul rest in peace! His Lordship had gone with me in the morning for a farewell visit to the Vatican galleries and their untold treasures.

Next morning, the third public Session of the Council was held. The fathers recorded their votes and the first decrees were passed.

The bishops wore red copes, and, as usual, the plain white mitre. The Pope delivered a very touching allocution, on the gospel of the day.

Monday, we witnessed the great procession—Rogation —from St. Mark's to St. Peter's.

In the afternoon we visited San Lorenzo *fuori le muro* where now rests all that is mortal of the great Pope Pius IX.

After supper, I finished the day by visiting the Bishops of Limerick and Galway, and the amiable Dr. Power, coadjutor of Killaloe, from all whom I had received the greatest kindness during my stay in Rome. Their lordships of Limerick and Galway, without any solicitation, gave me the most flattering letters of introduction to the clergy of their respective dioceses.

Indeed while life lasts I shall ever recall with deepest gratitude the unvarying attention, kindness, and I might even say affection, manifested towards me by those distinguished prelates. One, Mgr. McEvilley, is now Archbishop of Tuam—spoken of as a probable cardinal. The other two "now sleep their last sleep." "Blessed are the dead who die in the Lord." His Grace of Tuam, honored me with this letter in acknowledgment of the money sent to him from the noble congregation of St. Francis Xavier, Brockville.

ST. JARLATH'S COLLEGE, TUAM,
March 24th, 1880.

MY DEAR FR. MACCARTHY:—

Allow me to thank you most sincerely for your generous remittance of £103 st., which reached in due course, for the relief of the prevailing distress. You and your good flock shall have the prayers of our poor people fervently offered up for them.

I am very glad to have this opportunity of renewing our acquaintance. Well do I remember you, together with the good Dr. Horan. I think he and you were more with Drs. Butler, Power and myself than most any others; and you were always welcome visitors

I hope I may see you on the *green soil* to thank you.

Very sincerely yours,
† JOHN MACEVILLEY.

Very Rev. J. McCarthy.

Tuesday, April 26th—Got my passport for Florence. After dinner called at the Scotch College, and thence to the Strada-ferrata, the railway—to procure information regarding the trains. On returning, His Lordship accompanied me to the review of the young volunteers, by the Pope, which was held in the gardens of the Vatican. There was quite a gathering. His Holiness made a speech which was most enthusiastically applauded. He then distributed medals to the volunteers. As we left the gardens, I turned to take a last look at the great St. Peter's. Home, supper—a few hurried visits to friends, a long, long chat with my dear, venerable, saintly, and ever to be regretted Bishop; then to bed, to dream of Rome and its wonders, to which on the morrow I was to say 'adieu,' —probably for ever!

PISA.

WEDNESDAY, APRIL 27th.—Left Rome this morning for Pisa, in company with the Rev. Angus McDonell, of Prince Edward's Island. Exactly five months to-day since I reached the eternal city. Our way lay through Tuscany. We reached the city of the " Leaning Tower," about eight o'clock, passing through a delightful country and by the beautiful Leghorn, situated on the Adriatic, about half an hour's ride, by train, from Pisa. We put up at the Albergo di Londres, a very comfortable, but rather costly house, probably from being much frequented by the English, whom the Italians look upon as being all *meelords*, and of course, fleece accordingly. Next morning, a lovely day, we visited the famous leaning tower, something wonderful, the Campo Santo, or Cemetery, one of the most beautiful in Italy; the colossal Baptisterium, remarkable for its magnificent echo, and the grand old cathedral, rich in choicest paintings and costly sculpture.

SIENNA.

Sienna was reached in the afternoon. On our way, being delayed at Empoli for three hours, we had an opportunity to visit some very ancient churches. It—Sienna—is a fine city of some 26,000 souls, and beautifully situated in a hilly and picturesque country. It was here St. Catharine lived. We visited her house, and venerated the crucifix from which she received the Stigmata, or marks of the Saviour's wounds. St. Dominic's, St. Andrew's, St. Augustine's, St. Christopher's, and St. Peter's are all well worthy a visit. The cathedral, like most of the Italian cathedrals, is most imposing, entirely constructed of fine black and white marble.

The pavement of the church—Opus Alexandrinum—excels any I had before seen, except that of San Paolo, outside the walls of Rome. Beneath is the baptistery, containing a gorgeous font and the most exquisite bas-reliefs in bronze. The magnificent library, opening off the Cathedral—to the left—is richly frescoed; and the missals, breviaries, and antiphonaries shown us, exceed in brilliancy of coloring anything I had previously met; superior, I think, to those of the British Museum.

After the Duomo, or Cathedral, St. Augustine's is the finest church.

St. Dominic's has little to recommend it but its size. It contains twenty-three altars.

Going to Sienna we pass the pretty town of Certaldo, high upon the hills, and famous as the birth-place of the poet Boccacio, whose house, and the window of the room in which he was born, were pointed out to us by an Italian gentleman, evidently very proud of the glory of his countryman.

FLORENCE.

We slept at Sienna, and next morning left for La bella Firenze—beautiful Florence—arriving at noon.

The route from Empoli is simply enchanting. At Florence the Uffizi and Pitti palace attract all strangers, being a vast repository of paintings, statues, and the most exquisitely wrought gobelin tapestry imaginable. In this delightful city we visited the following churches : Santa Croce, in which are the tombs of Dante, Michael Angelo, and Galileo ; Santa Maria Novella, San Lorenzo, built in 340; San Marco, the Duomo, with its noble baptistry ; San Firenze, San Gaetano, Santa Maria Maggiore, and the Annunziata, the latter of almost incredible richness, ending in a superb rotundo, and dotted with a dozen altars. The dome is much admired for its beauty and elegant proportions. As we enter the grand door, to the left is the altar of the Blessed Virgin, entirely covered with the purest silver most exquisitely wrought. Crowds are always worshipping before it, and myriads of costly lamps burn ever about the holy shrine.

In the rear of San Lorenzo is the splendid octagonal chapel of the Medici, containing the tombs of that princely family. We drove considerably through the city, through which gracefully sweeps the Arno, alive with boats of every description. Next morning I said Mass at San Gaetano's, whose clergy received me most courteously, giving me the grand altar—quite a distinction. The following day was a special festival, and the good fathers urged us to remain.

In Florence we saw the house of the great poet—Dante, and the site of the dwelling of Americus Vespucius, from whom our own country takes its name.

PADUA.

Saturday we set out for Padua, crossing the Appennines, and passing through twenty-two tunnels on our route.

The highest point traversed by the train is 1,400 feet above the level of the sea. The scenery all through was grand and picturesque; indeed, often majestic. At Poretta, a small mountain village, we remained twenty minutes for refreshments—cheap and delicious. The little river Rheno flows here; the country seems well cultivated. The depôts along the line are prettily constructed and very neatly kept. We reached Padua about 8 p. m., and secured rooms at the Albergo della Croce d' Oro, taking our meals at the celebrated Caffé Pedrocchi, the finest in Italy.

VENICE.

"I stood in Venice, on the bridge of Sighs,
  A palace and a prison on each hand.
  I saw from out the wave her structures rise
  As from the stroke of the enchanter's wand.
  A thousand years their cloudy wings expand
  Around me, and a dying Glory smiles
  O'er the far times, when many a subject land
  Look'd to the winged Lion's marble piles,
Where Venice sate in state, throned on her hundred isles."

BYRON.

MAY 1st.—After celebrating Mass, we took the train for Venice, arriving there in one hour. Here we spent a most delightful day, visiting the principal attractions, and enjoying very much the charming novelty of the gondolas.

Venice is renowned for her splendid churches, rich and varied, and seemingly much frequented. We skimmed through the grand canal, our gondoliers doing their work most gracefully, and apparently very conscious of it.

We stood upon the Rialto; saw the Ponte dei Sosperi—the fatal bridge of sighs—the terrible dungeon; visited the palace of the Doges, with its galleries of the most exquisite paintings, and the wonderful Church of San Marco, the glory of the "Queen of the Adriatic."

This magnificent church is built in the Byzantine style. It contains a forest of marble columns, at least five hundred, and its walls are beautiful with forty thousand square feet of the costliest mosaics, upon a golden ground. From the Campanile—the great bell tower—316 feet in height, we had a splendid view of the city and for miles about it.

On the vast piazza of St. Mark, the pigeons are fed every day at 3 o'clock—at the expense of the city—a reward we believe, for services rendered by their *ancestors* —the carrier pigeons—to the republic in former times, when engaged in war.

After a most charming day in this enchanting city, we returned to Padua in the evening, and next morning I had the happiness of saying Mass at the altar immediately opposite to the tomb of the great Saint Anthony.

Padua enjoys a world-wide reputation for its great university, once attended by ten thousand students. St. Anthony's church is immense and very imposing; has rare and costly paintings, gorgeous stained windows, and the best organ I heard in Italy. The carving in the sanctuary is particulary fine. Beside the altar of the Saint stand two huge candelabras of fabulous worth, both in the material—solid silver—and workmanship. . They are placed on pedestals formed of a trinity of angels, of the purest white marble, and of the most elaborate design.

MILAN.

Monday we continued our journey to Milan, lunching at Verona, a noble city built on both sides of the Adige with a population of 65,000 souls.

A portion of the Quadrilateral, so famous in the Austro-Italian war, attracts much attention. As we went on we saw the commemorative tower of the battle-field of Solforino, whence Garibaldi was so shamefully driven by the Austrians. In the distance we gazed with rapture on the lovely "Lago di Guardi."

Travelling with us was a young sub-Lieutenant of the Bersaglieri, who spoke French very well, and who kindly described to us, as we passed, every object of interest along the route. His manners were charming; 1 could not but regret to see so fine a lad in the service of the robber-king, Victor Emmanuel.

At four, in the afternoon, we reached the city, the capital of Lombardy, and put up at the Hotel de la Grande Bretagne.

Next morning, the weather being delightful, our first visit, of course, was to the wonderful cathedral.

We ascended to the roof, enjoying a magnificent view. Mont Blanc, Monte Rossi, the Great St. Bernard and St. Gothard may, on such a bright day, be descried in the distance, their summits reaching to the skies, clad with eternal snows.

No pen, probably, has ever fittingly described Milan's great church.

Upward of five thousand white marble statues adorn the exterior; its top presents the appearance of a forest of pinnacles and spires of the most elegant and graceful form.

The "Duomo,"—as the Milanese call it, is said to have cost $160,000,000—more than twice the cost of St. Peter's. The plan occupied the architects for forty-six years.

In this great city I had the happiness of saying Mass at the grand altar of the ancient and elegant church of Saint Soteris.

Here, as everywhere in Italy, I found the clergy exceedingly polite and attentive.

Besides the Campo Santo—always an object of interest to the Catholic traveller in this Catholic land—the churches of San Sebastiano, San Ambrogio—famous in church history—San Vittorio, San Alessandro—the richest of all—and Santa Maria della grazia, deserve more than a passing call.

ON OUR WAY TO MUNICH.

MAY 3rd.—Lunched at Verona, and off again at 2 p.m., crossing the Alps, into Germany, by the Brenner Pass. The scenery, so often graphically described, is really magnificent. The Alpine peaks, the lofty mountains capped with eternal snows and dazzling in the rays of the evening sun; the lovely valleys highly cultivated; the spreading vines lining the way, and much advanced; the waving corn, the brilliant flowers, the lowing herds, the sheep, the goats, the shepherds in their quaint picturesque costumes, have an indescribable charm for the tourist through this lovely land.

With us, in the same coupé, was a young student from Virginia, United States. He was returning from the grand tour of Italy, to Germany, where he was pursuing his medical studies.

A most intelligent young fellow; he took in admirably all the sights, and was eloquent in his descriptions of what he had seen.

At Ala we stopped for refreshments, and went through the ceremony of having our baggage examined.

At Trent, Austrian Tyrol, we left the train for a few moments, just to be able to say our feet had pressed the soil of the little town, for ever rendered famous by the "Holy Council," to which it gave its name. The place is very quaint looking, of course, very German; lofty houses and high pitched roofs.

It was dark when we reached Innspruck, in the Bavarian Highlands. The night was very cold—such a change from the other side of the Alps—and considerable snow had fallen.

At the "Buffet" we had a glass of lager; not the wishy washy stuff—soap-suds and resin—one gets in this country, but like the "Dublin Porter"—*rale ateing and drinking*. The quantity is not stinted either: I fancied I should never see the bottom of the mug. The place was crowded; every one had a huge pipe in his mouth, and the clouds of smoke made me hurry out into the open air.

WEDNESDAY, MAY 4th.—We reached the royal city of Munich at half-past five this morning. We were exceedingly tired from our long ride from Milan, nearly twenty hours, and, having made a hearty breakfast—went immediately to bed.

During the day we "did the city," which is vast, handsomely laid out, and very beautiful in certain quarters. The cathedral is grand; the stained windows in all the churches are remarkably fine, in some, perhaps the finest in the world. During our stroll through the city we met the king, whom of course we saluted, and who in return most politely raised his hat.

Sitting beside His Majesty was an officer in uniform. A few attendants followed the royal carriage, which was drawn by four elegant black horses.

The king was in morning dress, and was paying an informal visit to the floral exhibition. His tragic end a few years ago, is still fresh in every one's memory. We left the capital of Bavaria next morning for Mayence, which is one of the great fortress-towns of Prussia. The cathedral is large, but cannot be called handsome; it was undergoing repairs.

It contains, among others, the tomb of the wife of Charlemagne. Being the Month of Mary, the usual devotions were going on in the evenings, in all the churches. We assisted at "Benediction of the Blessed Sacrament," and were charmed with the singing, in which the whole congregation, men, women and children joined, with admirable effect.

In Germany, music is taught in all the schools; so, all who pretend to sing, do so more or less well; hence, congregational singing passes.

In our country it would be hard to introduce the system without running the risk of making the singing ridiculous—at least for years. Even in our larger parishes it is difficult to bring together a dozen good singers. Were all to join in, probably they would be like the Widow Bedott's singers—kind o' independent—each one with a tune of his own.

COLOGNE.

May 6th.—Down the Rhine to Cologne. The boats plying on this famous river are in every respect worthy of it. The best of wines are kept on board, and the meals are excellent.

The whole world has heard of the glories of the Rhine. The most vivid description falls short of the reality. Like Naples, it must be seen to be realized. The scenery is among the finest that can possibly be imagined; the vine-clad mountains in the distance, crowned with the ruins of ancient castles, dating from the days of Roman power, give an inconceivable charm to the scene. At Coblentz, like the waters of the Ottawa and the St. Lawrence, one can easily distinguish the blue Moselle from the green waters of the Rhine.

A frowning citadel, reached by a bridge of boats, looks threateningly over the river.

We reached Cologne towards evening, and visited the cathedral, the most perfect specimen of gothic architecture in Christendom.

Its length is 511 feet by 230 in width. The spires were not completed—we believe they are now—and were to be 500 feet above the foundation.

There is a middle aisle and four naves in this magnificent temple, admittedly one of the grandest in the whole world.

There is a chapel here to the right, beneath the altar of which, tradition says, lie buried the three wise men of the East.

Nowhere have I seen streets so narrow. In some, one can scarcely pass the smallest conveyance.

Of course, others are broad and handsome; like at Milan, one is covered in with glass.

No one fails to see the church dedicated to St. Ursula, and its walls inlaid with skulls, said to be those of the ten thousand virgins—her companions.

We also saw here a large alabaster water-pot, said to be one of those used at the marriage feast of Cana—quite possible.

PARIS.

We travelled during the night, leaving Cologne at 10 p.m., and passing through Belgium, reached Paris early next day. Here we made quite a delay, visiting the principal attractions besides the Louvre, the Tuileries, the Bois de Boulogne, Pére la Chaise—the famous cemetery—the Jardin d'Acclimitation, the Champs Elysées, the Place de la Concorde, the Boulevards des Italiens, and many beautiful churches.

We said Mass twice at Saint Sulpice, and felt quite at home, knowing so well the gentlemen of St. Sulpice, Montreal, than whom the clergy have no better friends.

We went by rail to Versailles, and saw its gorgeous palace—the cause of so much misery to la belle France.

* * * * * * *

Paris is lovely, by gas-light—a fairy-like scene. The statues and paintings of the Louvre are beautiful; these galleries are always crowded, and with artists always copying. Here we saw many relics of the French Monarchs, from Childeric to Charles X., among which were the crown and sceptre of Charlemagne.

Of course we again visited Notre Dame, saw the Sainte Chapelle, and beautiful St. Roch's.

DOVER.

May 16th.—Reached Dover—charming crossing—and spent the night at my friend's Captain Moore's. My companion went on to London, where I joined him on the following day.

Our stay in London was short. We proceeded to Liverpool and took berths for America in the "City of Antwerp,"—Inman Line.

EDINBURGH.

Leaving Liverpool about 2.50 p. m., we reached Edinburgh, about nine o'clock, and put up at the hotel of the same name, Prince's street, and directly opposite Sir Walter Scott's elegant monument. It was a bright moonlit night; the view from the upper windows of the hotel was enchanting. Next morning, Sunday, we said Mass at the pro-Cathedral. Vicar-General Rigg, since Bishop, I believe, and Father Geddes, received us most graciously. The Bishop was in Rome, attending the Council. The pro-Cathedral is small, exceedingly plain and unpretending. The Empress Eugenie, when in Edinburgh, attended Mass in this church.

Edinburgh ranks with the first cities in Europe, and certainly commands one of the finest sites.

From Arthur's seat the view is magnificent, extending upon all sides, and across the Frith of Forth to the shores of Fife, and far out into the sea.

The castle is a point of great interest; and Holy Rood Palace of course has deeply absorbing attractions for the countless admirers of the beautiful Scottish queen, the loveliest of her sex; the good, the gentle; the unfortunate Mary Stuart.

We paid a visit to St. Margarets' Convent, where we were most kindly welcomed by the saintly and gifted Sisters.

Beneath their chapel—a sort of catacomb—they pointed out to us the receptacle in which had rested, for more than twenty years, the precious remains of Upper Canada's first bishop—the Hon. and Right Revd. Aléxander McDonell, to whom, and to whose nephew, *the Vicar-General*—Angus McDonell, the church of what is called Ontario to-day, owes more than to any other men; and whose names should be recorded in every Catholic church and institution in the land, as they should be enshrined in every Catholic heart.

We spent a charming day in this romantic city, of which the noble Scottish people are so justly proud. Its site is admittedly one of the very finest in all Europe.

INVERNESS.

Monday morning we started for Inverness, the capital of the Highlands, about twenty miles from Fort Augustus. The scenery about here is very beautiful, but the town, situated on the Ness river, is a dull, stupid place. From the fairies' hill, which is crowned with the cemetery, there is a very good view. This hill is remarkable, sloped like the bottom of a ship, and in length, wanting but a few feet of the " Great Eastern."

The Rev. Father Dawson was the Pastor of Inverness; like all the good fathers we met in Scotland, we found him exceedingly kind.

About Blair-Althole, the highlands are grand. As in all mountain scenery, many places are bleak and wretchedly barren.

We passed the historic fields of Culloden and Bannockburn; saw Stirling, with its fine castle; Perth, and the grand monument, near the latter place, erected to the memory of Sir William Wallace.

* * * * * * * *

On the train we met an old gentleman—a McDonald, of course—and of Capoch. Learning my companion was a Scotchman—and a McDonald into the bargain; that I was from Glengarry, Canada, and both of us priests—he happened to be a Catholic—he overwhelmed us with attentions, and begged us to come and "bide with him for a fortnight." I presented him with a little statue of the Blessed Virgin, which I had brought from my far off Canadian home, as a little souvenir. He raised his hat, pressed the image of Our Lady most fervently to his lips, and after a moment, said, "that shall go in the coffin wi' me."

* * * * * * *

We saw the famous pass of Killiekrankie; passed Dunblane, but didn't get even a glimpse of the "Flower."

GLASGOW.

It was near dark when we reached Glasgow; the evening was most inclement.

We supped at the Bishop's, with the Vicar-General, Father Monroe.

Glasgow, 43 miles from Edinburgh is the third city of Great Britain in population—395,000. It is noted for its commerce and vast manufactures—situated on the Clyde, it enjoys rare facilities for ship-building.

By train we went to Greenock, taking steamer for Belfast, Ireland, reaching there early next morning. This city is at the head of Belfast Lough; has a population of 120,000; is handsomely built, well kept, and apparently a place of great prosperity. It is noted for its linen manufactures, and enjoys a large foreign as well as domestic trade. Having seen all we wished of Belfast, we continued our journey to Dublin and Cork, visiting in each place the objects of greatest interest.

At Glasnevin, we stood uncovered before the tomb of O'Connell, and breathed a fervent prayer for the eternal repose of the illustrious dead.

We made a special visit to Blarney, its castle and its groves and, must we confess it?—kissed the stone. It was labor in vain—the stone must have lost its efficacy—at least the gift of blarney was not imparted to us. But perhaps 'tis as well—"an honest man is the noblest work of God." It may not always promote one's earthly interest, but it's much to look back to. It comes next to being "Innocens manibus et mundo corde."

AMERICA.

At noon, to-day, May 23rd, 1870, we left the harbor of Queenstown, for our own dear land. The return was delightful; the ocean so calm, the whole journey might have been made in a bark canoe.

We reached Halifax, my native place, on the 31st, and Boston, on Saturday, 2nd of June.

Sunday, the trains not going through, was spent at St. Albans, where I said Mass and preached, and left early next morning for Montreal.

* * * * * * * *

WEDNESDAY, June 5th, I returned to my dear old home, Williamstown, meeting with a most cordial reception, at the hands of all—Protestant and Catholic. Here as well as since—in Brockville—Protestants have been some of my best, my truest friends.

My visit to Europe, occupying just eight months, was perfectly delightful—satisfactory in every respect—a joy for ever.

And now, after many years, I look back still to it with feelings of intense pleasure, yet, more and more convinced of the truth of the words of the old familiar song:

> "'Mid pleasures and palaces, though we may roam,
> Be it ever so humble, there's no place like home."

FINIS.

NOTES ON THE MISSION OF SAINT FRANCIS XAVIER.

BROCKVILLE, COUNTY OF LEEDS, ONTARIO.

THE Mission of Saint Francis Xavier now comprises the town of Brockville, and takes in a portion of the surrounding country, extending to Maitland, on the east, Lyn, on the west, and Addison, in the rear.

Until September, 1884, St. James' Church, Yonge, was under the care of the pastor of Brockville, but since has been formed into a new mission, having been for about a year and a half attended by the priest assistant at St. Francis Xavier's.

The first priests attending the Brockville Mission were the Reverend Fathers Reynolds, Campion, Clarke, and the very Rev. William P. McDonell, Vicar-General, who for some years so ably conducted the *Catholic*, a religious weekly paper, published at Kingston and Hamilton, in the interests of the Church.

We know not the date of the building of the old church, now used as a separate school house for the boys, but we know that Mass was celebrated in it by the Right Rev. Alex. McDonell, when it could not boast of a floor other than the bare ground afforded.

The saintly Bishop sometimes said Mass at the residence of the late Dr. Hubbell, on Main-street, where now stands the fine building lately occupied by the MacNamara, Bros., as a dry goods establishment.

On looking over the old records of the "Mission," we find the first baptismal entry, dated the 17th day of December, 1835. Father Philip O'Rielly was then in charge. His last entry is on the 8th of March, 1847.

Some of the books show arrears of pew rents, going back as far as 1833.

Father O'Rielly's remains are buried at Kitly Church.

The first entries in the register by the Rev. Oliver Kelly, are in 1845.

The present church, one hundred and sixty-two feet long, by sixty-two wide, was begun by the last named priest, and the corner stone was laid on the 16th day of July, 1856, feast of our Blessed Lady of Mount Carmel, by the Right Rev. Patrick Phelan, Bishop of Carhœ, and apostolic administrator of the diocese of Kingston.

Father Kelly was succeeded in December, 1858, by the Rev. Henry Byrne, through whose untiring efforts, the church was closed in, and put in condition for holding divine service.

During his time, the "Devotion of the Forty Hours" was established, and a new impetus given to the confraternity of the holy scapular. Indeed, Brockville, owes much to this self-denying, devoted, zealous, Catholic priest; honored, respected, beloved by all.

The Rev. John O'Brien, for years the distinguished and venerated director of Regiopolis College, was named in 1864, to Brockville, by the Right Rev. Bishop Horan, as successor to the Rev. Henry Byrne, who, owing to ill health, arising from being thrown from his sleigh, had resigned.

J

The first entry on the parish registry by Father O'Brien is dated January 12th, 1865. This illustrious priest, afterwards bishop of Kingston, paid off a very heavy debt on the church; finished the plastering, put in the pews, and hung in the tower the splendid bell 3,100 lbs weight—one of the finest in the Dominion. By unceasing care he raised the schools to a degree of efficiency unknown until his time. Being named to the See of Kingston, the mother church of Ontario, he was pleased to appoint the Rev. Isaac John MacCarthy, then serving the mission of Williamstown, Glengarry, pastor of his own beloved Brockville, the latter taking charge on the 20th day of April, 1875, the very day after the consecration of the new bishop.

No parishoners ever more lamented the departure of a pastor than did the people of St. Francis Xavier's, that of Father O'Brien; and assuredly, seldom was a new bishop ever more welcome to a priesthood and people, than was the Right Rev. John O'Brien, to the priests and people of the diocese of Kingston. Learned, eloquent, saintly; beloved by high and low, rich and poor, never did the future seem brighter for a prelate. But the ways of God are inscrutable. A little more than four short years, and the "beloved of God and men" is suddenly struck down in the very prime of life, and torn from a devoted and inconsolable people.

During the eleven years and three months, the period of Father MacCarthy's incumbency, the generous and ever zealous people of Saint Francis Xavier's effected a very great deal. Besides most liberally providing for their pastor, and occasionally for an assistant priest, maintaining the services of their parish church in splendor, they built a parochial house—the finest in the diocese—valued, with its dependencies, at $9,000, and surrounded with grounds most artistically laid out.

Two properties were purchased for the use of the Sisters of the Congregation de Notre Dame, whom Father MacCarthy introduced in the autumn of 1878, costing about $12,000.

They also subscribed most generously towards procuring an establishment for Sisters of Charity; a work that fortunately has since been realized.

Three bazaars—not to speak of other efforts—yielded over $15,000; the last and third during Father MacCarthy's time, bringing in nearly seven thousand dollars, probably the largest amount ever made at a Catholic parish-bazaar, up to that time, in Canada.

A SUCCESSFUL BAZAAR.

(From the Brockville Monitor, published by John McMullen, Esq.)

The bazaar recently held in aid of the fund of the separate schools of Brockville, proved an immense success, as the card of thanks, published elsewhere by the ladies interested, shows. Mrs. John Murray's and Mrs. P. Cavanagh's tables, for which there was a working staff of seventy-five ladies, returned the large sum of $3303.42. The convent ladies, who had a helping staff of forty-six, came next with $1268.15.

Mrs. Delaney's table, with an assistant staff of twenty-seven ladies, returned $1135.45. Mrs. John Ryan's table, which had five lady assistants, returned $581.50. The refreshment table produced $275.30, and the door receipts $191.05.

The grand total of the whole receipts was $6,844.25 ! ! !

If the members of St. Francis Xavier's Church have bazaars only at long intervals (the last was held about four years ago), they manage by their unity and great industry to make them wonderfully successful. They will now be able to do a great deal for their schools (already in a flourishing state), and put them in a most excellent shape. They have certainly a *tower of strength* in their worthy and popular clergyman, the Rev. Father MacCarthy, who has done so much to elevate their educational and social status since his advent in Brockville. They owe that gentleman a deep debt of gratitude for all the admirable work he has accomplished in their midst.

(From the Montreal Gazette.)

The ladies of Brockville have realized the handsome sum of nearly $7,000 by their bazaar in aid of the Catholic schools of that city. The bazaar was under the patronage and direction of Father MacCarthy, parish priest of Brockville, whose popularity and active assistance lent no little aid to this gratifying result.

Eight teachers, five nuns and three seculars, conduct the schools, frequented by over four hundred children.

His Lordship the Right Rev. J. V. Cleary, S.T.D., the present Bishop of Kingston, visited Brockville in June, 1881, for the first time, and was greeted with a magnificent reception; all—Protestants and Catholics—vieing to do honor to the new bishop, and at the same time, show their love, respect and veneration for their parish priest.

The altars, frescoing, five stained glass windows, valued at $3,000—were obtained during Father MacCarthy's time; and the old church completely renovated and most commodiously fitted up for the male department of the separate school.

The Scapular, Living Rosary, Temperance and Holy Family confraternities flourished; the membership of the latter amounting to nearly five hundred. This society met every Wednesday evening at 7.50, for rosary, instruction and benediction.

The annual devotion of the "Forty Hours" was kept with much splendor; a large number, generally 800 approaching the sacraments.

One year there were six thousand communions.

The Young Men's Catholic Literary Association was much encouraged, and proved a real blessing to the parish.

A branch of the Catholic Mutual Benevolent Association was established, with an excellent membership.

Two missions were given during Father MacCarthy's pastorate, and proved eminently successful. Rev. Father O'Loughlin, a most accomplished and gifted preacher, conducted the first, of course, with Right Rev. Bishop Cleary's permission; the other was given by the Rev. Oblat Father Barber, who visited the whole diocese.

REV. FATHER MACCARTHY'S JUBILEE.

(From the Brockville Evening Recorder.)

FRIDAY, June 22nd, 1883.

On Wednesday the Catholics of this town celebrated the Silver Jubilee, or 25th Anniversary of their pastor, Father MacCarthy's elevation to the priesthood.

On the preceding evening, the reverend gentleman and a few friends were entertained by the school children, under the direction of the nuns, at a dramatic and musical soiree.

The efficiency with which the programme was carried out, testified to the ability of the nuns, and to the care which had been bestowed on the children's training.

On Wednesday morning, at the High Mass, which was sung by Rev. Father MacCarthy, the choir of St. Francis Xavier's rendered in happy style for the first time, the celebrated *Messe Bordelaise*— the leading part being creditably sustained throughout by Mrs. Shields. In the evening, the services were opened by the choir singing Lambillotte's "*Quid retribuam.*"

Rev. Father O'Loughlin then preached a magnificent discourse on the "Dignity of the Priesthood."

It is quite true to say, up to this, probably nothing surpassing this sermon had ever been heard within the walls of St. Francis Xavier's.

Solemn benediction then followed. One of its pleasing features was the execution of Zingarelli's "*Laudate*," by the pupils of the convent schools.

Great credit is due to Miss Caroline Braniff, for her excellent interpretation of the lengthy solo, which she sang with much feeling and spirit.

The *Te Deum* concluded the religious portion of the day's solemnities.

The committee of gentlemen of the congregation then proceeded to the gate of the sanctuary, where Mr. John Murray read the following address to Rev. Father McCarthy :—

REVEREND AND DEAR FATHER,—We, the members of the Presentation Committee, approach you on this 25th anniversary of your ordination to the priesthood, to offer you, in the name of your flock, whose representatives we are, our united congratulations, as the outward expression of our sincere participation in your solemn joy, together with a small token of our great esteem for your personal and priestly qualities, and a sincere, but inadequate, tribute f our deepest gratitude for the many blessings which under heaven your pastorship has conferred upon us.

A quarter of a century has elapsed since the imposition of consecrating hands made you a "priest for ever, according to the Order of Melchisedech,' and the unstained record of your sacerdotal and pastoral career evidences, on one hand, the omniscience of God; on the other, the fitness of the candidate whom He chose from among thousands on that eventful day to be the representative on earth of His Divine Son and His helper in the sublime work of Redemption.

You may look back with feelings of no mean pleasure and gratification upon the long roll of years that separate you from the auspicious morning of your ordination.

Your causes for joy and your titles to our esteem are manifold. Suffice it to single out for our respect your character as a gentleman, and for our love and veneration, the higher qualities which, as priest and pastor, you so eminently possess.

Your unobtrusive manners, polished deportment and genuine politeness have won for you the esteem, not only of your co-religionists, but of members of all denominations, in every section of society.

The ease of access which you furnish, your equanimity of temperament, your punctuality in engagements, and the acumen you bring to bear on matters subjected to your judgment, have enabled those who have had business relations with you, to pronounce it not merely a pleasure but a privilege to deal with you.

But it is chiefly in the discharge of your pastoral duties that your sterling qualities come to the surface, and your fitness for the high office you hold, is revealed.

The labors of your predecessors, it is true, had bequeathed you a magnificent temple; but you, Rev. Father, by well directed efforts, by a rare display of good taste, by a careful selection of ecclesiastical appurtenances, in a word, by judiciously pressing the arts into the service of God, have made it still more worthy of Him.

While they, your predecessors, might with a lawful pride, point to the memorial of their successful exertions and exclaim to the beholder: *Monumentum si quæris, aspice!* you with a no less legitimate pride and pleasure may indicate the various useful and artistic improvements you have effected in its interior, and exclaim in the words of the Royal Psalmist, "I have loved, O Lord, the beauty of thy house!"

The scrupulous cleanliness which in the church you enforce by word and example entitle you to appropriate the conclusion of that ardent apostrophe, "I have loved the place where Thy glory dwelleth."

Your faithful, intelligent and practical interpretation of the mystic and impressive ceremonial of the immortal Church of God in her functions and services, the result of careful ecclesiastical training, evinces the deep and loving faith which animates you in your holy and awe-inspiring treatment of the Divine Guest who dwells on our altars.

In this respect, we say it without fear of contradiction, the church in which you minister and we worship, compares favorably with every other in the diocese.

The order and decorum with which, in accordance with the apostolic injunction, the ceremonies and divine offices are carried out, have taught us to realize the saying of the great St. Augustine, "Order leads to God." The solidity of your instructions which, as the exponent of God's mind and word, you address to us from the pulpit and in the sacred Tribunal, the unction of your language, the earnestness of your delivery, make it manifest that they come from a loving heart and the well-garnered store-room of a cultivated mind.

This well deserved eulogium would be very incomplete were we to pass over in silence the interest you have always taken in the important matter of education.

By your action, more than by your language you have impressed upon us the truth, which in our days especially cannot be too often and too forcibly inculcated, that science is only one and that the lesser half of education. Your motto has ever been that of the Catholic Church, the civilizer of nations, "*In Sanctitate et doctrina*"—"Holiness before knowledge." The combination of both, but the paramount importance of the former, is the only true basis o education in its true sense.

Hence both in your former and present parishes you introduced the consecrated handmaids of the Lord and entrusted to them the training and education of our daughters.

With what complete success, the superior attainments and modest deportment of the children, the satisfaction of the parents, and the unbiassed opinion of all abundantly proclaim. All this and more, forces on us the conclusion that you were providentially chosen to fill the place of your worthy predecessor, our late lamented and revered Bishop.

We pray, then, dear Father, that you may be long spared to us as our pastor, to share in our joys and griefs, to be, as heretofore, our prop in adversity, our guide in difficulties, our influential model in the paths of life. We sincerely hope that time—*edax rerum*, as the poet says, may deal gently by you, and that when another quarter of a century shall have passed over us, your silver jubilee may have been succeeded by a golden one, and that we may be here as to-day to share in your joy and to offer our congratulations and the tribute of our life-long gratitude.

Signed on behalf of the congregation,

Hon. C. F. Fraser, Michael McGlade,
John Murray, T. W. Downey,
Patrick Cavanagh, John Ryan,
Thomas Braniff.

To which Father MacCarthy replied:

My Dear Friends,—It is with feelings of no ordinary pleasure that I have received your address on this auspicious occasion—the twenty-fifth anniversary of my elevation to the sacred order of the priesthood.

So well aware am I of your sterling qualities, of your generosity and goodness of heart, of the affection and devotion the Catholics of Brockville have entertained always for their priests, and the many proofs I myself have had of all this during the past eight years, make it impossible for me to say you have taken me by surprise.

I know your worth, too long and too well, to wonder at your kindly action on this thrice hallowed day.

Since my appointment by the Right Reverend Dr. O'Brien, whom I have had the honor to succeed in the care of this lovely parish, I have found you, my cherished people, all I could desire; affectionate, loyal, true, and generous beyond measure; ever willing to act on my suggestions—almost anticipating my wishes, and ready always to work with me and to second my every effort in the interest of our holy religion, and the grand cause of Catholic education. To you then, after God, with much thankfulness, I acknowledge I owe the brilliant success to which you so graciously refer, which has crowned my labors in your midst, and which gives St. Francis Xavier's so proud a place among the Catholic churches of the Dominion.

Nor, my dear friends, are these mere assertions. The thousands that you have given and which I have expended on your noble church; on the elegant parochial residence; on the schools; and lastly, on the magnificent house and grounds lately acquired for the use of the accomplished and devoted ladies, who, so carefully, so religiously, and so ably instruct our little girls, without any invidious distinctions, all bear me out in saying you have on all occasions most generously and most effectually assisted me; and that to you indeed is to be attributed the glory of that which has been done.

The costly gift accompanying your eloquent address

was not needed to convince me of your love and veneration —dearer far to me than its precious metal and glistening gems.

However, often will it remind me of this bright day, when so many, and such valued friends met together, offering at the foot of the altar of God, their heartfelt wishes and fervent prayers, for my temporal and eternal welfare.

I accept it then with unfeigned gratitude, assuring you that the proceedings of this solemn festivity—as pleasing to me as they are creditable to this parish—shall be another link in the golden chain binding me, if possible, more closely to my beloved people, whose interests in the future, as in the past, shall have ever the first claim upon me.

Again, my dear friends, I beg to assure you of my lasting gratitude ; to offer to you the expression of my perfect thanks, and to say, I find it very difficult indeed to command language which will express with sufficient earnestness, my deep sense of the kindness of which I have been the honored recipient to-day.

BROCKVILLE, June 20th, 1883.

The presentation was then made to the Rev'd. gentleman, of a magnificent chalice and set of Breviaries.

The chalice is of solid silver, chased in gold—the nodus is encrusted with amethysts, and the foot ornamented with a silver cross set in brilliants.

The Breviaries (4 Vols.) are solidly bound in Russian leather, and interleaved with colored and other miniature engravings, taken originally from the illuminated missals of the Middle Ages. The commemoration of this Silver Jubilee with its harmonious proceedings, constitutes one more link in the long chain of affection and esteem which unites the Catholics of Brockville to their worthy Pastor.

Many beautiful offerings were privately presented by individual members of the congregation.

The address, in book form, was bound in crimson morocco, richly gilt and splendidly illuminated. The Hon. C. F. Fraser, always a fast friend of the Rev. Pastor, and formerly one of his pupils in Regiopolis College, had seen to the preparing of it in Toronto. It is a credit to the eminent illuminators.

In May, 1885, his Lordship, Bishop Cleary, visited the mission and confirmed 147 persons, ten of whom were converts. He arrived on the afternoon of Ascension Thursday and remained till Monday following.

During his visit an address was presented in the Church, on behalf of the congregation; another at the rooms of the Catholic Literary Association; and one at the convent, where a very pleasing entertainment was given in His Lordship's honour. In fact, all entering into the spirit of their pastor, who by word and example always endeavoured to surround the episcopal dignity with the greatest respect, did their utmost to make this visit memorable among the events of the Brockville Mission.

His Lordship, in replying to the address from the pulpit, assured the people of his regard and good will towards them. He extolled the pastor, speaking of him in the highest, most flattering terms, and assuring the people that, "if he did not come to their parish oftener, the reason was—his presence was not required there. Some parishes he visited two and three times a year; but everything was correct in Brockville—they knew it and he knew it—therefore he did not deem it necessary."

His Lordship's remarks gave intense satisfaction, not only to the large congregation present, but to the entire parish.

AUGUST, 1886.—His Lordship was pleased to remove the Reverend Father McCarthy to another mission. The whole parish most respectfully begged the Bishop not to do so. Protestants and Catholics alike were deeply grieved at the decision. An address was forwarded to Kingston, signed most numerously by the best people of the town, without effect.

Finding Father McCarthy had but a very short time to remain in Brockville—in fact that he was to leave next morning—an address was hurriedly prepared, and a purse of $500 presented to him the same night.

The following is from the town daily papers:—

(Daily Times.)

A DESERVED TRIBUTE

PAID TO FATHER M'CARTHY ON LEAVING BROCKVILLE,

By his former Parishioners, who testify in tangible manner the esteem in which they held him.

When it became known to the congregation of St. Francis Xavier's Church that His Lordship Bishop Cleary had decided upon removing the Rev. Father MacCarthy from the parish of Brockville, a deep feeling of regret was expressed at his departure by people of all classes and creeds.

For eleven years Father McCarthy has ministered to the spiritual needs of those belonging to the Roman Catholic Church in Brockville, and during that time he has won the respect and esteem of all.

So strong was this feeling that it was felt that the occasion of his leaving could not be allowed to pass without, in some way, giving tangible evidence of it.

Accordingly yesterday morning a number of his friends set to work and during the day raised the handsome sum of $430, with which to present the reverend father. Had there been time this sum could have been largely augmented.

The presentation took place last evening. The members of St. Francis Xavier's Church, to the number of about two hundred, assembled in the rooms of the Catholic Literary Association, and proceeded thence to the residence of his sister, Mrs. Shannon, where Father MacCarthy was staying.

Here they were tendered a hearty reception and made as comfortable as possible. Rev. Father MacCarthy was then called to the front, when Mr. John Murray, read the following

ADDRESS.

The Rev. Isaac J. MacCarthy:

REV. AND DEAR SIR,—In view of the fact that our petitions and entreaties have been unavailing, and that we are unable to retain you as our parish priest, we feel, in gratitude for your past kind ministrations, bound to meet you here this evening and express to you our deep and heart-felt regret at being *compelled* to be parted from you.

We feel *that your removal is a calamity to us*; and when we consider what you have accomplished within the comparatively few years that you have been in the parish—for instance the schools, the convents, the presbytery; the embellishing and near completion of our beautiful and spacious church, and many other minor things, all of which bear witness, and are standing and living monuments of your energy and zeal, well may we feel that for a while your absence may prove retrogressive, but we trust in God, and hope it will be for our mutual good.

Not only do we feel your loss as a parochial worker and partaker of our wants and daily vicissitudes, but we feel that we have lost a friend and a father, one in sympathy with us, and always anxious to promote our temporal as well as spiritual welfare, in fact, dear father, we feel as orphans.

In our bereavement, however, we know that though separated, you will think of us often, and not cease to implore the Almighty God to shower His blessings upon us all.

It is a great consolation to us, as we are assured it is to you, to know of the unanimity of feeling and of love which this entire congregation entertains towards you, and, in leaving us, we can assure you that many an eye will moisten, and many a heart will throb and swell with painful emotion; in a word, you carry with you to your new home the love and esteem and the confidence of the whole parish.

As an evidence of our sincerity we herewith present you this purse. Though small in amount, it is nevertheless a token of our regard and our gratitude, as well as an acknowledgment of our filial affection. May God bless you.

BROCKVILLE, Aug. 27th, 1886.

Rev. Father MacCarthy replied in appropriate and most affecting terms, thanking them for their remembrance and invoking the divine blessing upon them in their future lives.

As stated before, the present was a purse containing the handsome sum of nearly $500.

Father MacCarthy has been twenty-eight years in the ministry. For seventeen years he was in the parish of Williamstown. He then came to Brockville, and has been here eleven years.

He now goes back to again take charge of the Williamstown parish, and carries with him the best wishes and kindest regards of the people of Brockville, Catholic and Protestant alike.

The names of the gentlemen that signed the 'Requisition' to the Bishop will be found on another page at the end.

From the *Recorder*, 27th August, 1886.—Rev. I. J. MacCarthy, late of S. F. X. C., was in town to-day bidding his host of friends farewell. He leaves to-night for Williamstown, and takes with him the earnest regards and best wishes of the people of Brockville, irrespective of creeds.

POPULAR PASTOR.

(*Practical testimonial to the Rev. Father MacCarthy.*)

(*Recorder, August 28th, 1886.*)

In no more striking way could the R. C. citizens of Brockville have shown their devotion to their late pastor, Rev. I. J. MacCarthy, and their regret at his removal to Williamstown, than in the way they did last night.

Learning that he was in town bidding adieu to old friends, and that he intended taking his departure by the early train this morning, they at once commenced preparing for him a suitable testimonial.

There were only a few hours in which to do the work, but that it was done well is apparent from the fact, that before 8 o'clock last night a handsome address and a purse containing $432.25 had been in the hands of those who originated the movement.

Shortly after that hour a meeting was held in the rooms of the C. L. A., when a procession, including about two hundred gentlemen was formed. The party proceeded to the residence of the reverend gentleman's sister, Mrs. Shannon, Victoria street, where the presentation was made, Mr. John Murray reading the address.

* * * * * * * *

Knowing the spontaneous nature of the testimonial, and recognizing the spirit in which it had been presented, the reverend gentleman was naturally filled with emotion, but in a feeling manner testified his appreciation and gratitude.

The address was nicely gotten up, reflecting much credit upon the gentlemen charged with it.

(*From B. Monitor, July* 16*th*, 1886.)

The Rev. Father MacCarthy—Very few men of Brockville have ever occupied as large a place in the affection and esteem of their respective congregations as the reverend gentleman, whose name heads this paragraph, but not only is F. MacC. esteemed by his own congregation, but also by the whole community. His exertions in behalf of his own people have been most unremitting and most successful; and their social standing to-day among the community, is a long way above what it was when he took charge of his present parish. Under these circumstances his approaching departure from amongst us cannot fail to be a matter of deep regret to a large number of persons, and we sincerely hope the change will be a better one for him.

We believe that his new position has not yet been assigned to him, but we hope that it will be such a one as he certainly merits at the hands of his ecclesiastical Superi ,r, the Bishop of K. The regret caused by his leaving Brockville will be greatly heightened if there is any disappointment in that direction.

(*From B. Monitor, Sept.* 3*rd*, 1886.)

The Bishop of his diocese having finally decided to remove the Rev. F. MacC. from B. to W., the members of his recent congregation on last Monday raised a purse of $430, and presented him therewith on the following evening, and also with a most feeling and affectionate address, expressing their deep regret at parting with him. Father MacCarthy deserved it all.

During the eleven years he has passed in Brockville he did much valuable work for the people, in various ways, and leaves them in a much better and higher position every way than he found them.

Father MacCarthy had charge of the Williamstown parish for seventeen years before he came to Brockville, and no doubt his former congregation there will gladly welcome him back again. We have been on the most friendly terms with the reverend gentleman during his residence here, as well as with his various predecessors down to Father Kelly, and deeply regret his departure from amongst us.

He is a perfect gentleman, every inch of him, and we wish him all manner of good as regards his future career.

(From the Kingston News.)

"The Rev. Father MacCarthy, who has recently been removed from Brockville to Williamstown," says the Kingston *News*, "was presented with an address and a purse of $432.25, by his old parishioners on Friday evening. The presentation was spontaneous, having been got up on the day it was made, and showed, no less than the petition recently presented to the Bishop against his removal, the very high estimation in which the reverend gentleman was held in Brockville. The address speaks of Father MacCarthy's removal as A CALAMITY to the Roman Catholic people of Brockville."

SIGNATURES APPENDED TO THE REQUISITION PRESENTED TO RIGHT REV. BISHOP CLEARY, FROM BROCKVILLE.

Hon. C. F. Fraser, M.P.P.
John Murray.
Michael McGlade.
O. K. Fraser.

J. Venney.
Timothy Burns.
Thomas McGrath.
David Aubié.

A. D. Leelair.
John C. O'Donohoe.
Henry Mathon.
James Gallagher.
Miles Bourke.
Nelson Beach,
T. H. Fitzgibbon.
I. D. Barsalow.
A. H. Franklin.
James Daniels.
J. P. Mervin.
J. I. Curran.
Joseph Belisle.
J. Godfrey.
M. Hussey.
John Marron.
John Cotton.
James H. Kelly.
Thomas Doyle.
M. C. Kehoe.
John Muldoon.
Martin O'Connor.
James O'Mara.
P. Cavanagh.
E. Loftus.
Timothy Burns.
P. Sweeney.
Dennis Monahan, Sen.
Patrick Connors,
John Ryan.
Edward Yorke.
R. Tessier.
Sylvester Donohoe.
Angus Belisle.
Michael Bradley.

Thomas McCord.
Edward Yorke, Jr.
John S. Fraser.
R. M. Ryan.
Fred Steben.
W. J. Jento.
D. Bradley.
William Maloney.
Jas. Bradley.
Owen Sheridan.
Thomas Sheridan.
John Toole.
T. Murphy.
Frank Blane.
M. Carmody.
George Troy.
Patrick Hunter.
John Coskern.
Jonas Morris.
James Lowry.
Murtough Mahoney.
John Yorke.
Oliver Belair.
Joseph Aubrey.
Thomas Brady.
William Meehan.
John McCord.
Thomas Burns.
James Burns.
John Boland.
Martin Mullen.
John Kelly.
John Duquette.
Jeremiah Goyette.
John Mackey, Sr.

James Vaney.
R. C. McHenry,
Michael Campbell.
P. J. Venney.
P. Derosier,
A. Clement.
Thomas Donohoe.
Felix Brazeau.
W. Blane.
Charles Peppin.
Patrick Finn.
Wm. Driscoll.
John McGovern.
Timothy Walsh.
P. Hart.
Joseph Fitzpatrick.
I. J. Doyle.
W. J. McHenry.
O. E. Liston.
W. J. Peppin.
James Shaw.
P. O'Donohoe.
D. W. Downey.
Harry Sheridan.
James R. Bresnan.
Mark Mullen.
John Burns, Sen'r.
Thomas Burns.
Dennis Burns.
John Burns, Jun.
William Cooley.
Edward Horan.
Thomas Burns, Jun.
James Burns.
James Farrell.

James Blair.
James Halpin.
M. P. Halpin.
Peter Poulin, Jr.
Stephen Ryan.
John Gallagher.
Dennis Gallagher.
Patrick Vanney.
Dennis Marron.
Daniel Crowley.
W. Wilkinson.
J. V. Tony.
G. H. Tony.
P. Rourke.
J. Crowley.
Richard Dugan.
John Whelan.
John M. Harper.
P. H. Flynn.
John Ford.
W. T. Jento.
John Sharkey.
R. Monahan,
Albert Lachapelle.
Louis Lachapelle.
J. P. Byrne.
Edward Young.
Thomas O'Brien.
Napolean Poulin.
J. Hurley.
William Braniff.
M. F. Gilmartin.
Charles Cato.
W. C. Reynolds.
Charles Hurley.

John Burns.
James Burns.
William Meehan.
James McCord.
P. J. Murray.
Cornelius Stevens.
James Tracey.
Benjamin Aimond.
Peter Frazer.
Christopher Larocque.
J. Mallette.
A. Larocque.
Fred. Baker.
R. P. Cooke.
Edward Barry.
T. Fitzpatrick.
Raphael McNab.
Michael Ennis.
Patrick Ennis.
Michael Burk.
J. Reilly.
D. Marron.
E. Selef.
James Brown.
Peter Campbell.
Antoine Ranger.
Joseph Laurent.
Francis Bonehard.
Dennis Monahan, Jr.
B. F. Hobart.
Alfred Tereault.
S. J. Geash.
Patrick Dillon.
John MacKey.
William Siclair.

John Taylor.
Thomas Taylor.
John Lacey.
James Barnes.
P. O'Neil.
Charles Hurly.
John Cleary.
Moses Lacasse.
George Graham.
John Casselman.
Michael Casselman.
P. J. Daley.
G. F. Byrnes,
Joseph Buler.
Terrence McGuire.
E. P. Roche.
W. C. Franklin.
Edward Franklin.
John Marron, 'Jr.
William Marron.
B. Phillips.
W. Lawson.
Hugh McSloy.
John McSloy.
Hugh McSloy, Jr.
Moses Sauvé, Jr.
Joseph Sauvé.
Noer Sauvé.
David Frigan.
Joseph Frigan.
W. Quinn.
John Franklin.
Charles Hurly.
T. Reilly.
M. Sullivan.

Timothy Jento.
William Larocque.
Frank Barrett.
P. H. Ryan.
R. H. Lindsay.
Paul Viance.
Wilson Wade.
C. Jento.
John Spellman.
W. J. Bradley.
Daniel McParland.
John Sheridan.
James H. Grant.
Moses Birtch.
Cornelius Connell.
James Fletcher.
Michael Carmody, Jr.
Dennis Troy.
Edward Hunter.
G. H. Lindsay.
M. O'Donnell.
James Cavanagh.
N. Cavanagh.
Charles L. Bertrand.
John Bennett.
Alex. Burshaw.
N. Labelle.
Ezra Aimond.
William Morton.
Charles Therault.
Elie Pariseau.
John Larocque.
M. Curry.
Thomas Curry.
William Curry.

T. Ennis.
W. Brassoe.
W. Sauvé.
William Fraser.
Henry Best.
H. Martin.
E. Martin.
E. Leavett.
William Manly, Jr.
B. M. Parland.
P. M. Garvey.
Henry I. Taylor
Patrick McHugh.
J. McGegor.
James McHugh.
P. Higgins.
A. Reilly.
G. Bertrand.
F. J. Delaney.
T. Lunney.
P. Daley.
John O'Connor.
Alexander Sutherland.
P. B. MacNamara.
Jules Girardin.
John Easton.
Patrick Ennis.
D. J. Brady.
J. Bissonette.
James Driscoll.
James H. Hall.
John Halleday.
N. McMullin.
Martin Hayes.
Maise Sauvé, jr.

A. Brown.
E. Maher.
C. Lunny.
James McGwyre.
M. Young.
M. Cleary.
John Monahan.
F. Mallette.
M. Thomas Braniff.
A. G. Manny.
W. S. Manny.
M. J. Webb.
R. McGrory.
Michael Costello.
Nicholas Baulf.
Denis Baulf.
Michael Kenny.
John J. Kenny.
Patrick Kenny.
Michael Kenny, jr.
James H. Russell.
Thomas Doyle.
M. Ryan.
James Connors.
Denis Bradly.
Michael Brady.
John Brady.
Patrick Brady.
John Sullivan.
Patrick Sullivan.
Thomas Dion.
John Ranger.
Nelson Lacasse.
John Hunter.
John Mellon.

Thomas McCormick.
Stephen Burke.
M. J. Screen.
M. Carey.
M. P. Toole.
John Belisle.
Joseph L. Thompson.
David Patrick.
George E. Shields.
John C. Bann.
John O'Keefe.
John McMahon.
M. J. Ritchie.
R. Driscoll.
Moses Brabant.
T. E. Martin.
Louis Mallette, jr.
George E. McGlade.
Frank Pierce.
James Braniff.
Patrick Gleason.
John Faro.
W. P. Driscoll.
E. A. Driscoll.
John Young.
Julius Mallette.
Wm. Bowman.
M. Sauvé.
William Webb.
Patrick Gallagher.
W. Ennis.
John D. Young.
P. C. Currie.
M. G. Kelly.
Thomas Curry.

James Mellon.	George Hutton.
B. Champagne.	J. B. Gerard.
J. Martin.	John J. Phelan.
John Brady.	George Morency.
Denis J. Brady.	J. Duquette.
Walter Bourke.	Fred Lesperance.
Charles Sauvé.	E. O. Sullivan.
Thomas Whelan.	Louis Malette.
William Muldoon.	Andrew Brabant.
Edward Kelly.	James Mellifont.
Thomas Brady.	James Toro.
Thomas Kelly.	Ernest Morency.
Thomas McGrory.	J. V. Morency.
W. H. Pinnock.	John Manny.
A. A. McGannon, M. D.	Patrick Cavanagh.

BROCKVILLE, Aug. 25th, 1886.

N. B.—Ladies were not asked to sign the "Requisition." Had time permitted to ask them, not a dozen men in Brockville—Protestant or Catholic—would have refused their names. Father MacCarthy's last bazaar is proof of this assertion, it bringing nearly one dollar *per head* for every man, woman and child of the then population, a thing unheard of in Canada since or before.

CHRISTMAS, 1886.

Though absent, Father MacCarthy was not forgotten by his Brockville parishioners at New Year's. A well filled purse reached him by express on the 6th of Jan., 1887. Neither was he overlooked at Xmas, 1887.

COMPLIMENTARY.

The reverend the Redemptorist Fathers from Toronto, gave a "Mission," extending over several days, at Saint Francis Xavier's, in the summer that Father MacCarthy left, and before its close, the reverend director spoke these significant words:—

"I have preached 'Missions' all over the United States and elsewhere, and from the lisping child, to the old man tottering on the brink of the grave, I have never met a better instructed congregation."

Laudetur Jesus Christus, in aeternum.
AMEN.

"DIES IRÆ, DIES ILLA."

AS

(Translated by Father MacCarthy.)

O day of days, O day sublime,
Eternity opening, ending time,
In ashes lays this world in fine.

Oh! the terror! Oh! the dread;
The Judge Supreme of quick and dead,
His wrath pours out like molten lead.

The wond'rous trump with awful sound,
Re-echoes far—is heard around,
Mankind summoning from the ground.

Death itself—and nature too,
Hearing, trembling at the view;
The past, the future shuddering rue.

Seated, weary, Thou did'st me wait,
By Thy cross, O Jesus great,
Be not in vain Thy suffering state.

Thou the Judge of heavenly ire,
When guilty mortals shall expire,
Save me from avenging fire.

Sinful man! in grief I pine,
Crime has dyed this soul of mine;
Yet hoping ever in mercy Thine.

Thou who did'st the Magdalen raise;
And the thief of blood-stained ways;
To Thee, honor, glory, praise!

Unworthy are these prayers of mine;
But lovingly Thou dost incline
To suppliants seeking mercy Thine.

The fatal book is open spread;
Mortals cowering, hear it read;
Sentence is passed on living and dead.

The Judge is mighty, stern, severe;
Before Him all men must appear;
Nothing shall be hidden here.

Wretched!—what can I then say,
On that sad, eventful day,
When earth and heaven shall melt away?

King of awful majesty!
Saving us in sheer pity;
Font of love! do Thou save me,

Mindful ever, Jesus good,
That for us upon the rood,
Thou did'st shed Thy precious blood.

Among Thy sheep grant me a place,
Rescued from that dire disgrace ;
Oh ! may I gaze upon Thy face.

Prostrate on the earth I lie ;
Heart-bruised, stricken, hear my cry ;
Jesus, for me Thou did'st die.

Trembling, weeping, lowly bending,
Man awaits that day unending,
Heaven and earth asunder rending.

Oh ! the day of bitter tears ;
Oh ! the night of endless years ;
The Judge amid the clouds appears,
The world, mankind, all disappears !

Saviour, Jesus ! Thou the blest,
To our souls grant peace and rest.
      AMEN.

"THE CRADLE SONG OF THE B. VIRGIN."
Translated from the Latin by Father MacCarthy.

Sleep, my darling, sleep,
 Thy mother sings to thee ;
Oh ! sleep, my boy, my treasure
 Upon thy mother's knee :
Ten thousand, thousand angels
 Will chant thy lullaby.

Sleep, sweet heart, thy mother's throne !
 'Tis thy mother's jubilee ;
What on earth, or in heaven's home
 Can sweeter, holier be ?
While angels, yea ten thousand,
 Cry out in ecstasy.

> That nothing may be wanting,
>   Thy couch with lilies fair
> I'll strew, and roses, blushing roses,
>   Shall perfume the midnight air;
> While angels, guardian angels,
>   Will protect us with their care.
>
> Would'st music?—gentle shepherds,
>   With strains so soft, so sweet,
> The echoes of the heavenly host
>   Thy infant ears shall greet;
> While angels, yea ten thousand,
>   Will sing: "'Tis just and meet."
>
> Brockville, Christmas, 1885.

INSTRUCTIONS FOR ST. PATRICK'S DAY.

MARCH 17th, 1885.

Delivered on St. Patrick's Night, by Father MacCarthy, at the Sacred Concert given in the church, for the benefit of the Poor of St. Francis Xavier's Parish, Brockville, Ont.

"Behold, I have given thee to be the light of the Gentiles, that thou mayest be my salvation to the farthest part of the earth."—Isaiah, Chap. 49.

Among the Saints of God, to none, beloved brethren, can the words of the Prophet Isaiah be more fitly applied than to him whose festival we celebrate this day. *Chosen by Heaven*, St. Patrick brought the light of faith to our pagan ancestors, and in the mercy of God has been His salvation to the extremities of the earth. Of him, well may it be said, "The just shall be in everlasting remembrance." And did inspiration require proof, no other need be asked than the solemnity which assembles multitudes this day throughout the world;—a solemnity dear for a thousand reasons to the hearts of the millions of Ireland's fair women and brave men.

Memory of a just man.—Whose memory is it, my brethren, that is so honored on this festive day, the world all over? It is the memory of a just man, a sainted bishop, an apostle who was given to be the light of the Gentiles, a hero of the noblest stamp, whose life was consecrated to the service of God and of his fellow men; who, full of years and merit, having fought the good fight, having finished his course, was called to his reward more than fourteeen hundred years now gone, and whose glory still fills the Catholic world. "The just shall be in everlasting remembrance." Yes, dearly beloved brethren, the name of St. Patrick is held in highest honor and reverence in every country, in every clime. In every quarter of the globe Irish Catholics are found, and on this hallowed day, their generous, grateful hearts shall beat with love at the mention of their National Saint, and their tongues will sing his praise; while on hundreds of altars, a faithful priesthood, the successors of his virtue and his power, will offer to the eternal, living, and true God, the adorable sacrifice, in thanksgiving for the favors and blessings granted to our glorious patron and apostle.

How did St. Patrick merit this remembrance?—But how, I ask, has St. Patrick merited this everlasting remembrance? His zeal for the glory of God; his triumph over paganism; his apostolic labors; his conversion of the Irish nation were, my brethren, the origin of his worldwide fame; the secret of his glory, the source of that immortality which, according to the Sacred Scripture, shall be limited only by eternity: " The just shall be in everlasting remembrance."

387.—The year three hundred and eighty-seven was distinguished by the birth of our Saint. His parents were illustrious by their rank, and still more by their sanctity and holiness of life, which indeed constitute the only true claim to true nobility. Captured by Neil, a daring Irish prince, Saint Patrick was brought, like another Joseph, into the land whose saviour he was destined to become, and sold as a slave. Often, beloved brethren, misfortunes overwhelm us; shadows cloud our path; burdens are laid upon us, almost too great for human shoulders to bear. But let us remember, God strikes but to heal; the passing trials and cares of life, the miseries incident to all stations and ranks must, if borne with submission to the Divine will, eventually conduce to our best and dearest interests for time and eternity. It were impossible to tell the sufferings of St. Patrick during his long and wearisome captivity. But God watched over him, and in this school of adversity perfected the future apostle of Ireland. His sufferings at length terminate; his bondage ends; and a friendly vessel carries him back to the home of his childhood.

Return home.—Fair France once more presents itself to his straining eyes. Its coast now breaks upon his sight. What feelings must have crowded his youthful breast, now that after years of exile, worse than death, he is again to press the vine-clad hills of his native land. Now that after years of suffering and captivity he is once more coming back to the home of his fathers, dear to him by so many and such holy recollections. More than all, now that he is again to behold that loved mother who first taught his infant lips to utter the sacred name of Jesus, that name which, in the providence of God, he was destined to announce to the Irish nation, then buried in all the horrors of idolatry and superstition.

Returns as a Bishop.—But time rolled on. Years had passed since his departure from the land of his captivity, and now he returns invested with the power and authority of a Bishop of the Church of God. Sent then, as now by the only legitimate spiritual authority on earth, by the Vicar of Christ, by the successor of St. Peter, by St. Celestine, the Pope then gloriously reigning, gladly and courageously he undertakes the conversion of the Irish nation.

Lands at the mouth of the Boyne.—Landing from his frail bark at the mouth of the Boyne, that ill-fated river, he proceeds to Tara, and, like St. Paul confronting paganism on the hill of Mars, the Elect of God boldly attacks the pagan priests and princes, in presence of the Ard-Righ, the chief monarch of the Isle. St. Patrick met with little opposition. No Roman pro-consul had ever set his foot in Ireland. God had preserved the people from the vile influences of Roman corruption. Roman profligacy had never blighted or tainted the land, and when Christianity was offered to Ireland, she had not to oppose to it, as a bulwark, the habit of vice and of a shameless immorality. She embraced the new faith with ardour; as an Irish poet has said, "With the sudden brightness of a northern summer." Convinced by his arguments, the best, the noblest in the land are converted and regenerated in the saving waters of baptism. Victory follows victory, the death-knell of druidical superstition had sounded; the day of idolatry is gone for ever; and Ireland soon becomes the island of sages and of saints.

Fifth Century.—The fifth century was well nigh spent, and the sands of life were numbered for our great Saint. "Franks ruled mighty in the Netherlands; Britain, to the south, lay crushed beneath the Saxon heel. The Rhine knew another bank when the chivalrous Clovis led his followers into Gaul; and vandalism reigned supreme in Spain and Northern Africa, while Italy, lovely Italy, the fairest of God's earth, was a prey to Ostrogoths. A polytheistic empire had been succeeded by barbarism, and not even ignorance could be offered in extenuation of the darkness that overspread the semi-Christian countries of the old Roman Empire." My brethren, Europe was hastening to its destruction. But God's work never fails. A light still flickered; "the smoking flax still smoked, and the bruised reed was not yet broken."

A Sun Arose.—The Saviour dying on Calvary's gory mount, let drop his head to the West; and in that West arose a Sun almost as brilliant as on the morning of the God-man's resurrection. It rose o'er the emerald isle of the ocean, enlightening Europe, and dispelling the more than the midnight gloom that had shrouded Saxons,

Franks and Germans in worse than Egyptian darkness. From Rome, Alma Roma, a benefactress then, as now, a light had shone upon Erin; and not surpassed by even Rome, Erin reflected the light, and reflects it even to this day to the ends of the earth. "Behold, I have given thee to be the light of the Gentiles, that thou mayest be my salvation to the farthest parts of the earth." From Erin shone forth the bright light that illumined the growing darkness of the rest of Europe. She was, as a celebrated writer says, the quiet habitation of learning and sanctity. Ireland was the school of Europe. Strangers flocked to her for instruction; and from her bosom went forth native students in all directions, as teachers and missionaries, diffusing learning and science, and heralding the glad tidings of salvation. No fewer than eight nations must acknowledge that it was on the altar of religion in Ireland they lighted their torches and brought back faith and piety from our country to their own. Irish learning was found in the seminaries of the continent, as afterward Irish statesmanship was found in her cabinets, and Irish valor in her camps.

Death of St. Patrick.—The year 493, beloved brethren, saw the death of the sainted priest, of the aged bishop, of Patrick the Apostle of Ireland, one of the greatest of the saints of God. His first Easter in Ireland he spent at Tara, and then, in presence of the king, and all his tributary princes, nobles and priests, he kindled that material fire which the king did not extinguish; which Druidical foresight foretold as prophetic of rule in Ireland. A fire truly emblematic of that spiritual fire which the

Apostle came to light, which Christ came to cast upon earth, and which was never to be extinguished in Ireland. On St. Patrick's arrival in the land of our fathers, it was in an humble shed he offered the adorable sacrifice of the Mass. Here—and it was meet—now the site of the noble monastery, he gives up his soul to God.

Honors surrounded his tomb; and then, as now, for priests and Christian people prayers were said, masses were offered, and tapers burned so constantly about his tomb, that the gloom of his death seemed changed into a glorious light that was destined to shine to the extremities of the earth. "Behold, I have given thee to be the light of the Gentiles, that thou mayest be my salvation to the farthest extremities of the earth."

Let us now glance for a moment at the wondrous results of the mission of St. Patrick, and see the deep root, the one, holy, Catholic and Apostolic faith took in the fertile soil of the great Hibernia.

Ireland's eagerness to receive the faith.—No other nation ever received the faith with such eagerness, and to Ireland's glory be it said—no other has ever guarded the Sacred deposit so zealously and so well, though for ages it has pleased heaven to allow her to be persecuted, aye, crushed beneath the iron heel of monsters incarnate; for, though the Catholic Church was established in the land of our fathers without bloodshed, yet, and alas! unfortunately torrents of blood were shed for her destruction. The very thought of Ireland's sufferings for God and for His church is enough to freeze the blood in our veins and make us hang our heads in shame for our common humanity that could have conceived such diabolical cruelties. Scarcely did the tyranny of Pagan Rome, in the heyday of her greatest infamy, inflict more terrible tortures upon the early Christians, than were inflicted upon the Irish people for the twofold crime of being faithful to the one true faith and to the One true God. And never did the world behold greater heroism, greater devotion, greater constancy than they invariably displayed. All that the malice of hell could suggest to its minions incarnate was done in order to destroy the Church and uproot the faith planted in the Island of Saints by our glorious apostle, more than fourteen hundred years ago. Ages, yes truly, dark ages of blood, and slaughter and persecution; torments in every shape and form; the gallows, the rack, fines, imprisonment, exile, death; all failed, miserably failed in their hellish object. Sacred edifices were destroyed; priests were hunted like wild beasts—a price being set upon their heads; and still the eternal priesthood survived, yea, grew strong in persecution; and the foundation of the Irish Church—the One, Holy, Roman, Catholic and Apostolic Church—the Church of Christ; the Church of Peter, of Patrick, of Gregory, of Pius, of Leo XIII. of the Saints of God, against which the gates of hell shall never prevail, was for ever cemented in the blood of her martyred people.

Danes and Saxons fail.—For well nigh fifteen hundred years, "Ireland steadily, heroically and conscientiously has held the Catholic faith;" as a modern writer tells us, "for three hundred years the Danes endeavored to change that faith into paganism; for the Danish war was a religious war." Ireland fought, fought with heroic strength, fought with unfailing arm; fought with undying, though bleeding heart, and for three hundred years she struggled until at length she cast the Dane to the earth, and then Christ put His foot on the neck of the pagan Thor of the Scandinavian.

"Another three hundred years came, and it was no longer the Dane, but it was the Saxon that held his sword at the throat of Ireland and said, even as the Dane of old had said: Paganism or death! So the Saxon said to her: Protestantism or death; and Ireland answered as she had answered the Dane: I will suffer, I will fight, I will die; all this I know how to do and well; but my faith I never will change from God, from His Christ and from His holy Church. And just as after three hundred years of war, on that Good Friday morning, the sun rising in the heavens beheld an Irish king and his Irish army stand in triumph, pealing forth their songs of victory over the prostrate and fallen Danes; so after another three hundred years, the sun rose on that fair May morning in 1829, and beamed upon the face of the great O'Connell, and the Irish nation, waving over the ruined battlements of the old blood-stained Protestant law-established church, the glorious banner of religious equality and freedom which was to be ours for ever."

Even in our own day Ireland has suffered; and we have seen her people driven from their homes and their country, dying in thousands of starvation, while there was plenty in the land. And we know, my brethren, that heaven knows, and the world knows that a thing so monstrous had never been permitted had they not joined to the crime of being Irish, the still greater crime of being Catholic too.

God alone knows the tale of Irish wrongs. In the sacred archives of heaven alone can be found a true, faithful record of what Ireland has suffered for God and for His church. Man cannot conceive what she has undergone rather than abandon the faith once delivered to the saints. But, my brethren, " Revenge is mine, saith the Lord, and I will repay." Let us draw a veil over the past; let us forgive, and try to forget; remembering the "disciple is not above his master;" and that He for whose honor Ireland has suffered so terribly and so long, has declared them blessed who suffer persecution for justice' sake, assuring them, for such is the kingdom of God.

If, beloved brethren, with the eye of faith we regard the sad history of Ireland's wrongs—the blackest page of Europe's history—we shall see that all has been permitted for a wise, a good, a truly great end. Persecution and oppression, that no word in the English tongue can qualify, have scattered the Irish people to the ends of the earth. Go where we may, the faithful children of St. Patrick are found spreading the faith, establishing Christian schools, erecting altars to the living God; everywhere we find them a truly apostolic people—the advance guard of Catholicism, upholding that holy Church which our illustrious Saint bequeathed as a glorious inheritance to that lovely isle of the West, the emerald isle of the ocean; the home of soldiers, of statesmen, of scholars, of sages and of saints; the loved, the persecuted, the unconquered and the unconquerable Hibernia.

Position of the Church due to Ireland.—What would the Church be to-day among the people who speak the English tongue, were it not for Ireland and the Irish people? See England, Scotland, Australia, the neighboring Republic, and our own happy country, this Canada of ours; what I ask would be the position of the Church in these vast regions, were it not for Irishmen and their descendants. All honor to the noble Scottish Highlanders, and to the handful of true Englishmen who never bent their knee to Baal, who, amid persecution and temptation were ever faithful to their Church and to their God. All honor to them, but unfortunately they were few, too few to effect much—the nation in general had apostatised.

Yes, my brethren, Irish faith, Irish arms, and Irish hearts did God's work and did it well. Let us then rejoice as we celebrate this festive day; let us rejoice as we calmly behold the outcome of tyranny and oppression, terrible in themselves and stamping with eternal dishonor and infamy their vile authors, yet, children of St. Patrick, in their consequences glorious for Ireland and for you, since that tyranny and oppression have been followed by such magnificent results, beneficial to mankind, and increasing the glory of St. Patrick, the apostle of a Church, the spiritual father of a great people, that has given to earth heroes, to heaven saints, and which has ever been faithful to the Spouse of Christ, the bride of the Lamb, our holy Mother Church, despite the fiendlike malice of heresy, and the unjust, the cursed, the cruel policy of centuries of wrong.

St. Patrick thanks God.—Before the throne of God—the great white throne—St. Patrick thanks the Divine Majesty for Ireland's fidelity to the one, holy, Roman, Catholic and Apostolic Church, which neither lapse of ages, nor heathen rage, nor earthly temptations, nor all the arts of hell have been able to destroy; and, in turn let us thank God for giving Ireland so powerful a protector in heaven, such a model for earth. To-day our saint in glory untold sees God face to face. His soul is filled with ineffable delight, the reward of his saintly life and exalted virtues. And from his bright throne in heaven, methinks I hear him say: My children, be faithful unto death, even as your fathers have been. Be ever true to the holy Church. Cling to the grand old faith, once delivered to the saints, and without which it is impossible to please God. Obey your prelates, the bishops and priests whom God has placed over you, who have at heart your best interests. Never in your history has the *Soggarth aroon* proved false. Faithful when all others are faithless, you shall ever find him, as your fathers found him, devoted to you, heart and soul, for that devotion has its source in devotion to his God.

Be United.—Men of Ireland, be united! Remember union is strength. "The national spirit cannot exist, but with the aid and support of a strong will; and that which gives strength is union." United you will overcome every obstacle, dissensions will disappear, and success will crown your every undertaking.

"Irishmen," said O'Connell, "do you love your country? Well then, let there be no disorders, no troubles, no secret societies, no plots, no conspiracies against established order." Let us love our country, says a celebrated French writer, let us love our country such as it is, with its past as with its present; let us love it with its whole history; let us love its great men; its monuments of all ages; its beliefs; its traditions; its glory; all that it has bequeathed to us, all that our ancestors have transmitted to us from the cradle of history to our own days; let us not despise our fathers for what was wanting to them, but let us love them for what we have received from them, and let us carefully try to keep it, and add to it what is still wanting. Let us love our country; after God and His Church, it should be our best love, and the object of our dearest hopes. We know not what future awaits her, but reasonably we may hope her darkest days are gone, and for ever. Fondly do we hope the days of her ancient pride and splendor may soon return. "That the chains that hang around her may be broken;" that the turns in the fortunes of men, the changes of realms and the chances of time may soon restore her to her legitimate place among the nations of the world. "That the blood of her sons and the wealth of her soil may not have been lavished for ever in vain." Yes, earnestly do we pray, and sincerely do we believe that the day star is rising, the sun bursting forth, and that ere long peace, happiness and prosperity will be vouchsafed by a just God, to our beloved, most patient and long suffering nation.

O illustrious, glorious Saint! in terminating this instruction, it is to thee we direct our vows, our prayers. Our ancestors honored thee as their father; we are therefore thy children and have a right to claim thy powerful protection. Deign to receive favorably the heartfelt prayers which we address to thee this day for our beloved, though unfortunate country. Obtain of God that soon the clouds may be dispelled; that soon the sun of Ireland's glory may rise, never, never, to set again. But more than all else, obtain for thy children, for all who honor thy glorious festival, grace to serve God as thou has done, with such fidelity during life, that when they too shall have closed their eyes upon this world of sorrow and of sin, they may enjoy with thee in heaven, those ineffable delights prepared for them by a merciful God in a happy eternity.

AMEN.

NOTES ON THE MISSION OF THE NATIVITY OF THE BLESSED VIRGIN MARY.

WILLIAMSTOWN, COUNTY OF GLENGARRY, ONTARIO.

The late Right Revd. Patrick Phelan, Bishop of Carhoe, and Administrator Apostolic of the Diocese of Kingston, yielding to the urgent and oft repeated solicitations of the Catholics of Williamstown, Martintown, Lancaster, etc., etc., resolved on establishing a new parish, for that object taking a portion of St. Raphael's, which was very extensive, and entailing altogether too much labor on one priest.

The land for church, presbytery, and cemetery—four acres—was most generously donated by the late Hugh McGillis, Esq., who, as the tablet over his grave in the church has it, was an eminent benefactor to this parish.

This gentleman, and it should not be forgotten, in the days of Bishop McDonell, had offered to build a church here at his own expense.

His nephew, John McGillis, Esq., and his excellent family, continued for many years, until their removing to Montreal, to carry out the traditions of the uncle, by the unvarying interest they always took in the church and the welfare of the parish.

Mrs. McGillis, an accomplished musician, for many years presided at the organ; directed the choir, possessing a rare and highly cultivated voice, and also saw most scrupulously to the requirements of the altar.

The present substantial stone church, 85 × 52 feet, was commenced, and the supervision of its construction entrusted to the late Very Revd. George Hay, then pastor of St. Andrew's. The slab over the grand door bears the date—1849—with the inscription : " D. O. M."

The Church was blessed by His Lordship, Bishop Phelan, assisted by the Very Revd. Vicar-General, John McDonald of St. Raphael's ; the Very Revd. George Hay, St. Andrews ; the Revd. John McLachlin, Alexandria ; and the Revd. John Meade of Lochiel.

The cemetery, and the bell, the gift of John Hay, Esq., were consecrated the same day. The donor and Mrs. McGillis were sponsors for the bell. The first priest lived in private lodgings for a short time, until the completion of the presbytery—a small, but very comfortable brick cottage, erected at the cost of $2,000.

Four years had not quite elapsed when the Revd. Isaac J. MacCarthy, ordained on the 20th day of June, 1858, was appointed parish priest (not being yet 23 years of age), of Williamstown, by the then Bishop of Kingston, the Right Rev. Edward John Horan ; and entered upon his charge, September the first, of the same year.

The parish, not quite four years established, of course was anything but well organized. True, much had been done, but much more remained to do.

The first parish priest was the Revd. Francis McDonagh ; and the first entry on the parish register is dated October 20th, 1854. He was a model of neatness; his church was admirably kept.

The first collection made by Revd. Father MacCarthy

was for the purchase of the beautiful Statue of the Immaculate Conception that now stands over the grand altar. It was blessed on the 8th of December, 1858.

The following spring, 1859, Father MacCarthy, accompanied by Mr. John Hay, a devoted friend of St. Mary's, visited all the houses of the parish, soliciting subscriptions for the completion of the church.

This summer the side galleries were removed and another placed, as at present. The church was painted and tinted ; the outside walls pointed, and the organ purchased.

On the 18th day of September, 1859, His Lordship blessed and erected the Stations of the Cross. These Stations—the frames and the crosses are now in St. Joseph's Chapel, Lancaster—were formerly in the old St. Joseph's Church, Kingston, in the days of Bishop McDonell, Gaulin, and Phelan.

Bishop Horan gave them to Revd. Father MacCarthy, who had often, when a child, performed the Holy Way of the Cross before them.

(Extract from the Parish Register.)

On Sunday afternoon, September the 22nd, 1861, the remains of the Honorable and Right Rev'd. Alexander McDonell, first Bishop of Kingston, and of all Upper Canada, which were brought from Scotland, were conveyed accompanied by an immense concourse of people, from St. Raphael's, to St. Mary's Church, Williamstown.

They were received at the grand door by the Rev'd. Isaac John MacCarthy, pastor of the parish, assisted by the Very

Rev'd. Angus McDonell, V. G., nephew of the illustrious deceased, and the Rev'd. John Quinan of Tracadie, Nova Scotia.

The remains were placed on the Catafalque before the Altar, and the absolution was performed.

The next morning at 8 o'clock, a solemn High Mass was offered up, the Very Revd. the Vicar-General McDonell, being the celebrant, assisted by the Very Revd. Dean Hay, and the Revd. the parish priest, as Deacon and Sub-deacon.

The funeral oration was delivered by the Revd. John Quinan. The sermon being ended, another Solemn Libera was chanted by the Revd. the parish priest, at the conclusion of which the hallowed remains were borne to the neighboring parish of St. Andrew's.

Isaac John MacCarthy, P. P.

Witnesses to the above:

Very Revd. A. McDonell, V. G., Williamstown, Glengarry, Sept. 23rd, 1861.

Very Revd. John McDonald, V. G., St. Raphael's.

Very Revd. George Alex. Hay, R.D., St. Andrew's.

Revd. J. J. Chisholm, D. D., Alexandria.

Revd. John Quinan, P.P., Tracadie, Nova Scotia.

On the 17th day of June, 1863, was made for the first time, in the Parish of Williamstown, the public procession of the Most Blessed Sacrament.

The Canopy was carried by six gentlemen, viz: John McGillis, Esq, Laird; Angus McLellan, South Branch; John Hay, Gore; Duncan G. McDonald, Front; Archibald Grant, Front, and Peter Gadbois, Williamstown.

The lanterns, on east side of the Canopy, were carried by—Walter Barret, John Barret, John McRae, Angus Ban McGillis, Duncan McDonald (Martintown), and Thomas Heenan.

Twelve little girls, in white, strewed the way with flowers. Two Repositories were erected: one at Thomas Barrett's, and the other at the Laird's—John McGillis, Esq.

About two thousand people accompanied the Most Adorable Sacrament.

In testimony of the above, I hereunto affix my signature.

I. J. MacCarthy, Priest.

NOTES ON THE MISSION OF THE NATIVITY OF THE BLESSED VIRGIN MARY.

WILLIAMSTOWN, GLENGARY, ONTARIO.

(*Extract from the Parish Register.*)

(*The Devotion of the " Forty Hours " adoration.*)

September 8, 9, 10, 1862.

On the 8th day of September, one thousand, eight hundred and sixty-two, the devotion of the "forty hours " adoration of the Most Holy Sacrament, was established in the Mission of the Nativity of the Blessed Virgin Mary, of Williamstown.

His Lordship opened the devotion by a Pontifical High Mass, at which the Rev'd. Monsieur Marcoux, of St. Regis, and the Rev'd. Dean Hay, of St. Andrew's, assisted as Deacon and Sub-deacon. The other Rev'd gentlemen present were :—Canon E. C. Fabre, of the Cathedral, Montreal ; William Leclair, of the Seminary of Saint Sulpice ; B. F. Chôlette, of St Polycarpe ; J. J. Chisholm, of Alexndria, and John S. O'Connor, of Cornwall. This is the first Mission in the Diocese of Kingston where this devotion has taken place.

During it, eight hundred and fifty-three persons approached the tribunal of penance—and received Holy Communion. Eighty-three persons were confirmed, most of whom were adults.

I. J. MacCarthy, P.P.

St. Mary's, Williamstown.

On the first day of September, 1865, the Sisters of the Congregation de Notre Dame, from Montreal, opened their day and boarding school; so far (1887) the most successful academy in the Diocese of Kingston.

On Sunday, the 8th day of July, 1866, the Right Revd. E. J. Horan, assisted by the Very Revd. George Hay, and the Revd. François Marcoux, of St. Regis, consecrated the Grand Altar, the gift of John Hay, Esq., of the Gore, to St. Mary's Church.

In a letter, dated Kingston, 15th November, same year, 1866, to Revd. Father MacCarthy, His Lordship writes:

"In virtue of an Indult granted by the Holy Father, and dated Rome, 1861, empowering me to attach to one altar in each of the Missions of this Diocese, the indulgence of the *privileged altar ad decennium*, I hereby declare the High Altar in the Parish Church of Williamstown *privileged*, and attach to it the plenary indulgence of the *Privileged Altar* each day of the week until the 21st April, 1871.

"In order to give a mark of lasting esteem and grateful feeling to Mr. John Hay, who so generously contributed the funds for the erection of your beautiful altar, it is my wish that for fifty years, dating from this year, a Mass be said every year in the month of September, for Mr. John Hay and his family; the church of Williamstown is to pay the retribution for the Mass."

"Yours sincerely in Christ,

† E. J., BISHOP OF KINGSTON."

REVEREND WALTER BARRETT.

On the 10th day of July, 1867, the Right Rev'd. E. J. Horan, Bishop of Kingston, conferred upon the Rev'd Walter Barrett, Deacon, the sacred order of the Priesthood in presence of a large congregation, and the undersigned Rev'd. gentlemen. Rev'd. Father Staunton preached the sermon of the day ; a master-piece of pulpit oratory :

Very Rev. Dean Hay,	I. J. McCarthy, P. P.
Rev. John Masterson,	Rev. J. J. Chisholm, D.D.
Rev. M. Stanton,	Rev. John O'Connor.
Rev. E. Murray,	Rev. M. Lynch.
	Rev. Alex. McDonald.

On the 14th day of December, 1868, took place the funeral of Rev. Walter Barrett, priest, aged thirty-four years. His Lordship, Bishop Horan, assisted by the Very Rev. Dean Hay, as assistant priest, and the Rev'ds. M. Lynch and Alexander McDonell, as Deacon and Sub-deacon, celebrated the Solemn Requiem Mass.

The attendance was large. The church was draped in deepest mourning, and everything possible was done to show respect to the memory of the honored dead, whose loss was most sincerely deplored by all who had the happiness of being acquainted with him.

His remains, in a metallic coffin, are interred beneath the floor of the Sanctuary, on the gospel side, near where stands the pulpit.

May his soul, and the souls of all the faithful departed, through the mercy of God rest in peace.

October 23rd, 1869, Rev. Father MacCarthy left for Rome—Vatican Council—in company with His Lordship of Kingston.

The parishioners kindly presented him with a purse of $500.

He returned the following June, 1870, being absent just eight months.

M

The Sisters of Charity, from Kingston, made their first collection here, in the winter of 1869, realizing about $300 worth.

This same winter a 'Triduum' was held in Lent, by order of His Lordship the Bishop.

The beautiful New Stations—oil paintings—were purchased by Father MacCarthy, in Paris, France ; and, in virtue of faculties granted by Bishop Horan, were blessed and erected by him, in February, 1872.

This winter, during Lent—an eight days' Mission was preached by the Rev. Father Longcake, S. J.

NEW YEAR'S DAY, 1873.

On New Year's Day 1873, the ladies of the parish presented the Rev. Father MacCarthy with a magnificent gold watch. This was the sixth Presentation to this gentleman, by his generous and devoted people.

Midnight Mass had always been celebrated at St. Mary's, from the founding of the parish till Father MacCarthy's departure—discontinued after. The Confraternity of the Holy Scapular, the Living Rosary and Temperance Society were all in the most satisfacory condition.

The convent has been enlarged three times ; twice before Father MacCarthy left ; again since his return.

Father MacCarthy, in 1873, secured two fine lots for a chapel at Lancaster. When he left to take charge of the important Parish of Brockville, he had given the contract for the new church and, besides other disbursments on account of it, left in bank over $15-00, for the good work

This amount, with the proceeds of the pic-nic, decided upon before he left, and which came off in July, 1875, nearly sufficed to pay the entire cost of the building.

During Father MacCarthy's first occupation of the Mission, nearly ten thousand dollars were raised by him for parish improvements.

The Rev'd Charles Gauthier, on the advice of the Rev. Father MacCarthy, was named by His Lordship Bishop O'Brien, Pastor of Williamstown, April 1875.

The beautiful oil painting in the convent chapel, the Blessed Virgin and child, was purchased in Rome, and presented to the Nuns by Father MacCarthy on his return from the Eternal City.

Up to April, 1875, Father MacCarthy had married in Williamstown 185 couples; baptized 1220 children and adults; interred 444 persons. There were many converts during his time.

April, 1875, Father MacCarthy left for Brockville, to which parish, quite unsolicited, he had been appointed by the newly named Bishop, Dr. O'Brien. Venturing to demur a little with His Lordship, the latter answered, "If you don't come to Brockville you must go farther." This closed the matter, Father MacCarthy gratefully accepted the nomination to the lovely parish of Brockville, whose people, while with them, and since his removal from them, have always shown themselves most sincerely, most steadfastly, and most affectionately devoted to him. Years before the Right Revd. Dr. Horan had offered to Father MacCarthy the *Rectorship* of the Cathedral of Kingston. It was, with sincere thanks, most respectfully declined.

ADDRESS FROM THE PARISH.

To the Rev. I. J. McCarthy, *Williamstown.*

Reverend and Respected Sir,

It is impossible to describe, or even attempt to give utterance, to the great sorrow and deep regret that more than over-burdens the hearts of us, your Parishioners, by your departure from our midst. Links of spiritual love and Christian friendship, have formed a chain of unity between Priest and people, that we feel as if naught should sever.

Sixteen years !—yet it seems but a momentary dream—you, beloved Pastor, have graced the sanctuary of St. Mary's Church, Williamstown ; offering the adorable sacrifice, praying for our salvation, exhorting us to virtue, and urging us onward in the path of right.

Through your generous influence and untiring zeal, has our little "Temple of God," acquired its present devotional standing. Our convent, to you alone we owe its thriving condition. Our missions were established by your heroic self sacrifice. Our midnight mass, heralding the divine infant's birth ; our grand processions, edifying and orderly ; our "forty hours" before our dear Lord in His sweet sacrament of love,—all ! all these and innumerable other proofs, of your holy and energetic ministry, for *our welfare*, claim our unbounded gratitude.

And, we *are* grateful ! Yes, Reverend Father, we *are* truly and deeply grateful for your pastoral labors, your *saintly* example, encouraging counsels, charitable and generous works.

But, alas ! since you must leave us, rest assured the people of Williamstown Parish will treasure your memory with many a fervent, *God Bless Him.* We entreat you however, upon *every* occasion that your new duties will allow a leave of absence, to come and gladden us by your respected presence. A hearty welcome will await you each time.

Fain would we tender you, most worthy sir, a testimonial equalling our respect and love ; but such being impossible, we beg you to accept this purse of pure intrinsic value. It is at least a symbol of our numberless good wishes.

God grant you health, peace in fine, all manifold blessings, and should we forsooth never be permitted to have your constant spiritual guidance again in Williamstown, yet we confidently trust that the union which has been our anchor here on earth, may be our seal in heaven.

Your devoted and grateful children in Jesus and Mary.

THE PARISHIONERS OF WILLIAMSTOWN.

Williamstown, April 6th, 1875.

Recollections of Rome,

·FAREWELL.

TO OUR BELOVED PASTOR
REV. FATHER MacCARTHY.

From the Convent.

Our hearts were all joyous some short time ago,
   Forward we look'd to that thrice happy day,
When in the presence of our Father, we'd go,
   Our gratitude express, in accents bright and gay.
So sweet 'tis to tell the goodness of a friend,
   Whose sole desire was his fond children's weal;
But the smile and the tear do now slowly blend,
   While *all* seem to mourn, and sorrow to feel.

Our convent home looks sad and dreary now,
   That beloved home always so bright and fair;
A mournful look appears on each young brow,
   And joyous hearts are fill'd with doleful care.
But why these signs of sorrow 'neath our dome?
   Say why do joy and mirth give place to woe,
Has some *one* left our ever cherish'd home,
   Or say, if some *kind one* prepares to go?

Alas! *too true it is*, and sad to hear,
   A gentle *friend*, from us is call'd away;
Ah yes! from us is call'd our father dear,
   Whom we lament, on this thrice gloomy day.

Yes, belov'd Pastor, 'tis with hearts full sore,
   We would our deepest sorrow fain express ;
But *where* find words our sadness to deplore,
   In view of *all* thy loving tenderness,

Thou kind Father, who on us bestowed
   The precious gift that gold could never buy ;
Thou'st drawn us from a dark and dismal road,
   And plac'd us on the path that leads on high.
If the fount of science has been unseal'd,
   And in its streams our thirst we can allay,
To *whom*, if not our gentle Father's zeal,
   We owe that debt which we can ne'er repay.

Ah *yes*, lov'd *Pastor*, *guide*, and *Father* dear,
   Thy kind devotedness we've long enjoy'd,
Thy fond interest and paternal care
   Have fill'd our home with pleasure unalloy'd
But the sweet remembrance shall long remain
   Deeply engraven in each grateful heart,
And often we'll repeat, o'er and o'er again,
   Each kindly act which thou didst us impart,

Most worthy *Pastor* ere from us thou dost leave,
   Our sincere wishes we would fain express
Which as a bright garland, we'd fondly weave,
   Compos'd of sweet joy and true happiness,
Yes belov'd Father, our most fervent pray'r,
   And heartfelt wishes are sincerely thine ;
May thy future flock prove worthy of that care.
   And paternal love which in thee they'll find,

But we, thy children true, do fondly ask
   One sweet request which quickly strikes each mind—
To our convent home, as in days gone past,
   Sometimes a visit pay to *those* thou leav'st behind.

Ah yes! we hope that thou wilt ne'er forget,
    Thy truly fond and grateful children here;
Others thou may'st meet as good and loving, yet
    None with hearts more grateful or more sincere

Alas! comes the thought, *must* we say "*Farewell*,"
    Ah! the *sad, sad* thought, *must* we bid "*adieu*,"
To our father dear, whom we've lov'd so well,
    To our tender Pastor gentle and true.
Ah yes! but fondly hope that we'll meet again,
    After our convent home, in a home above,
Where there's no sad parting, sorrow nor pain,
    But where *all* shall be united around the *God of love*.

THE PUPILS OF THE CONGREGATION OF NOTRE DAME.

Williamstown, April 3, 1875.

FINIS.

LAUS DEO, ET MARIÆ IMMACULATÆ. Amen.

ERRATA.

Page 37, line 15, for "82" read "72."
" 40, " 11, after the word "John" insert a full stop.
" 48, " 23, for "Romulas" read "Romulus."
" 61, " 4, for "Jerome" read "St. Jerome."
" 102, " 10, for "Riheim" read "Righelem."

Ah yes! we hope that thou wilt ne'er forget,
  Thy truly fond and grateful children here;
Others thou may'st meet as good and loving, yet
  None with hearts more grateful or more sincere

Alas! comes the thought, *must* we say "*Farewell*,"
  Ah! the *sad, sad* thought, *must* we bid "*adieu*,"
To our father dear, whom we've lov'd so well,
  To our tender Pastor gentle and true.

www.ingramcontent.com/pod-product-compliance
Lightning Source LLC
Chambersburg PA
CBHW020904230426
43666CB00008B/1305